D1525629

On Suicide

DISCUSSIONS OF THE VIENNA
PSYCHOANALYTIC SOCIETY—1910

ON SUICIDE

With Particular Reference to
Suicide among Young Students

With contributions by

ALFRED ADLER, SIGMUND FREUD,
JOSEF K. FRIEDJUNG, KARL MOLITOR,
DAVID ERNST OPPENHEIM,
RUDOLF REITLER, J. [ISIDOR] SADGER,
WILHELM STEKEL

Edited by
PAUL FRIEDMAN, M.D., Ph.D.

INTERNATIONAL UNIVERSITIES PRESS, INC.
New York, 1967

Contents

3-25-69; 2.10; Swann

On Suicide

Acknowledgments

THIS TRANSLATION of the 1910 Symposium on Suicide was selected as a project of the Library Committee of the New York Psychoanalytic Institute in order that this unique document become accessible to English-speaking colleagues and students of psychoanalysis and related fields. I am grateful to Drs. K. R. Eissler and B. L. Pacella, my fellow-members of the subcommittee, for their invaluable cooperation.

First drafted in London by Mr. Edward Fitzgerald, who is well known for his translations of psychoanalytic literature. The text has since been revised several times. Every effort was made to convey the spirit of the original German. It is hoped that we have been successful in this endeavor.

I wish especially to thank the Peter Cats Foundation and the M. C. Schrank Foundation for providing the funds for this project.

P. F.

Foreword

THE YEAR 1910 was significant in the history of the psychoanalytic movement and equally so in the history of our thinking about the problem of suicide.

Its historical significance in terms of psychoanalysis lies in the very fact that this was one of the last meetings of the original group of associates at which Freud presided. Only a short while later, Adler and Stekel started the secession from the movement.

As for the evolution of our thinking about suicide, the year 1910 marked a definite turning point. Europe allegedly again witnessed a resurgence of suicide, especially among young people. Such epidemics had been cyclical for almost three centuries, and, each time, society had sought the motive forces responsible for driving human beings to self-destruction.

The mysterious demons of the Middle Ages

had provided a ready-made answer to the suicide problem, but subsequently they had been replaced by agents more in keeping with the thinking of the times. The scientific world of the early 1900's was imbued with a deterministic philosophy which looked to the outer world for all the causes of human conduct, even more so for the causes of suicide. Perhaps our resistance to psychological thinking can best be epitomized in the attitude of mankind toward suicide.

One example of this tendency to rationalize causation was evident following the publication of Goethe's romantic tragedy, *The Sorrows of Werther*. It was believed to have had such a powerful impact on young people that many committed suicide as did the hero of the book. And when, in 1903, Otto Weininger, the author of *Sex and Character,* put an end to his life at the age of 23, after completing this monumental work, it was again presumed that he had instigated a wave of suicide among European high-school and university students.

Thus the schools became the most vulnerable target for public attack and pedagogy was made the scapegoat for the self-destructive acts of young people. Challenged by such accusations, the educational world began a vigorous fight to defend its dignity. The teachers turned to science and to the social behaviorists for rescue.

The Symposium of 1910 was a most eloquent attempt to provide such an answer. It concerned itself with suicide of adolescent students. The main reporter was Professor Oppenheim, a teacher of classical languages.[1]

It is perhaps pertinent at this point to survey briefly the general cultural climate in which this Symposium took place. It was a climate in which the conception of external causation had changed in form but not in content, a climate in which suicide was seen as the result of and dependent upon immutable forces, conditions that are neither flexible nor capable of change but are inexorably imposed upon man and to which he must succumb. It was a climate over which the spirit of Montesquieu (Charles de Secondat, 1689–1755) and his *L'Esprit des Lois* still hovered, a climate in which suicide was believed to be caused by cosmic factors, an opinion not altogether alien even in the mid-twentieth century.

Such views of suicidal acts as being wholly

[1] Coauthor with Freud of *Dreams in Folklore* (1911). New York: International Universities Press, 1958.

In the original German text of the Symposium discussions, Oppenheim is referred to as *unus multorum* ("one among many").

contingent upon external causes unrelated to human will had led certain authors to attempt to formulate the laws governing suicide. The Belgian astronomer and statistician, Lambert A. Quételet (1796–1874), for example, looking upon the occurrence of suicide as an entirely constant phenomenon having no relation to the will of man, came to the pessimistic conclusion that the number of suicides is a fixed and immutable tribute laid upon humanity—a tax that is paid with frightening regularity.

The same determinism pervaded the medical sciences as well. The pathological anatomists, in particular, believed they had found the secret to the age-old mystery. For example, Julius Bartel (1874–1925), the Viennese pathologist, after numerous autopsies performed on suicides, arrived at the conclusion that the so-called *status thymicolymphaticus* constitutes a predisposing factor to self-destruction in every human being.[2]

When Bartel published his findings in 1910, a horde of researchers rushed to the corpses of suicides in order to detect those fatal stigmata. I still recall the first suicide autopsy I

[2] *Status thymicolymphaticus,* which the pathologist Paltauf (1872–1935) believed to be the cause of sudden death—*mors thymica*—is no longer considered a special pathological entity.

[14]

attended in 1926 at the Institute of Forensic Medicine of the University of Berne. It was a girl of eighteen, who died in a suicide pact while her fiancé survived. Although aware of the psychological theories on suicide, I examined the organs with the most careful curiosity, still expecting to find some of those mysterious stigmata in the "inside."

This is not the place to describe the lively discussions that ensued in medicine at that time; they were submerged by a controversy that revived the phrenological theories of the seventeenth and eighteenth centuries.

One is often tempted to ask whether the pathologists had completely forgotten that the corpses they dissected once harbored a "soul." Their approach is paralleled in present-day assumptions that chemotherapy and ECT can revolutionize human behavior and exterminate the "evil" mechanisms of the human mind and eliminate self-destructive impulses.

This relentless effort to assign the causes of suicide to external pathophysiological influences appears to be the rationalization of a deep-rooted resistance to explain purely human actions by the psychic dynamics of man himself. For man has, at all times, obstinately refused to search for determinants within his own self.

[15]

He has always preferred to rely in a quite primitive and magical way upon extrinsic supernatural forces. One may wonder whether certain speculative trends in contemporary research are merely new guises of old resistances.

Of course, of all the sciences concerned with suicide, psychiatry has been in the most favorable position to rationalize causation. For a long time, it was believed that the problem could be solved by diagnosing it as some form of madness.

Bourdin,[3] Esquirol,[4] Brierre de Boismont,[5] even Krafft-Ebing[6] and Gaupp,[7] all seem to have regarded suicide as an act of mental disorder—although Brierre de Boismont made a slight concession. He granted that among those who commit suicide there might be some whose minds are sound but whose "moral being" is impaired.

The most profound study was made by Esquirol. He, too, regarded suicide as an act committed in a state of acute delirium. Neverthe-

[3] Claude Étienne Bourdin (1815–1886): *Du Suicide Considéré comme Maladie*, 1845.

[4] Jean Étienne Esquirol (1772–1840): *Sur la Monomanie Suicide*, 1827.

[5] A. F. Brierre de Boismont (1797–1881): *Du Suicide et de la Folie Suicide*, 1856.

[6] R. von Krafft-Ebing (1840–1902): *Die Melancholie: Eine klinische Studie*, 1874.

[7] Robert Gaupp (1870–1953): *Über den Selbstmord*, 1905.

less, his way of viewing the problem was original and interesting. For instance, he emphasized the psychogenic character of suicide. Among the varied causes, Esquirol stressed social and environmental conditions in particular. Above all, he singled out the difficulties in the social structure that upset an individual's emotional and moral equilibrium and provoke disorders.

Esquirol's views as to the psychogenic and reactive character of suicide did not prevail for long. These theories were subject to vast and radical changes under the influence of the new developments in psychiatry. On the one hand, even greater emphasis was placed on the organotoxic origin of psychic disturbances; on the other hand, even greater importance was ascribed to hereditary and constitutional factors. Thus, psychogenic and reactive factors postulated by Esquirol came to be disregarded completely.

The sociological world of the time was still governed by the influence of Emile Durkheim (1858–1917) who had, at the turn of the century, published his classic study, *Le Suicide*. His theory, which was based entirely on the collective principle—the concept of a social suicide rate—can be summarized very briefly as follows. Two fundamental tendencies, which are inherent in any group or collective agency, create the conditions responsible for the phenomenon of "social suicide": the tendency to integrate its members into a whole, and the tendency to regulate their feelings and behavior. Any overintensification or weakening of these tendencies results in a specific type of "suicidogenetic current," and the intensity of this social current determines the "suicide rate" of a given society or group.

The very consistency of his conception, in which everything is reduced to the single factor of a "social element," led Durkheim into the pitfall he was bent on avoiding, unaware that his own view had become as one-sided as those he criticized and rejected.

Durkheim was critical of the philosophical and pessimistic approach of Quételet who held that the suicide rate, being based upon what he called the "average type," must be immutable in any given society. But he himself arrived at a hardly less fatalistic conclusion: "From this point of view there is no longer anything mysterious about the stability of the suicide rate, any more than about its individual manifestations. For since each society has its own temperament, unchangeable within brief periods, and since this inclination to suicide has its source in the moral constitution of groups, it must differ from group to group and in each of them remain for long periods practically the same. It is one of the essential elements of social coanaesthesia."

These inconsistencies and paradoxes in Durkheim's approach to the problem are not surprising to the psychoanalyst of today. They reveal how much the thinking of this original and keenly scientific mind remained colored by the universal resistance to psychological phenomena.

Indeed, the purely descriptive and nondynamic psychiatry of his time was incapable of serving Durkheim's evaluation of his remarkable observations and statistics. He was as critical of Esquirol's thesis that "suicide shows all the characteristics of mental alienation," and of its description as a "monomania" by Brierre de Boismont, as he was of Bourdin's theory which viewed it as a disease *sui generis,* a special form of insanity. "Clinical experience," he states, "has never been able to observe a diseased mental impulse in a state of pure isolation; whenever there is lesion of one faculty the others are also attacked, and if these concomitant lesions have not been observed by the believers in monomania, it is because of poorly conducted observations."

[19]

We may speculate that Durkheim would have taken a different position had he been acquainted with the subsequent contributions of psychoanalysis. Indeed, nineteenth-century sociology recorded a wealth of astute and valuable observations which have become meaningful only with the development of dynamic psychology. Thus, the statistical findings by Durkheim and the yet earlier works of Masaryk,[8] Ferri,[9] and Morselli,[10] which gave rise to great controversy, had to await this development to achieve their true significance.

This, then, is essentially the climate in which the Symposium of 1910 took place.

The following comments concern the individual contributions to the Symposium which laid the foundation for our psychological thinking about the problem of suicide. Not all of the ideas expressed by the participants can be considered psychoanalytic in the real sense of the term. Adler rightly stated that each speaker "necessarily" drew upon his own experience

[8] Tomas G. Masaryk (1850–1937; Philosopher and Statesman; First President of Czechoslovakia, 1918): *Der Selbstmord als soziale Massenerscheinung der Modernen Civilisation,* 1881. (Masaryk's assumption that suicide is a product of civilization and did not exist in primitive cultures has been disproved by modern anthropological findings.)

[9] Enrico Ferri (1856–1929): *L'Omicido-Suicido,* 1883.

[10] Enrico Morselli (1852–1930): *Il Suicido,* 1879.

and therefore the broad spectrum of ideas.

Adler pointed to the vengeful and impulsive acts of young people aimed at the punishment of parents. He, of course, applied his characterological principles to the dynamics of suicide and emphasized the "internal antagonism between submission and the tendency to instinctual gratification." But even the psychoanalytic aspects as formulated by Reitler, Friedjung, Sadger, and others may sound somewhat anachronistic and naïve to the reader of today. We must not overlook the fact that even the hypotheses formulated from real analytic and dynamic standpoints were derived from the chemicomechanistic conception of the libido theory still prevalent at that time. Hence—in the opinion of Reitler—it was the ungratified libido that was directly transformed into the examination anxiety of the young person which eventually led to the suicidal act.

Be that as it may, most of these ideas were truly revolutionary at the time they were first introduced. It was certainly unprecedented to cite psychosexual crises and heterosexual and homosexual conflicts as causative factors of suicide in youth. It was no doubt baffling in 1910 for Sadger to enunciate his all-encompassing view making Eros the sole prophylactic measure against suicide: "Nobody commits suicide," said he, "who has not given up the hope for love."[11]

But the most momentous and perhaps the boldest contribution to the 1910 discussion was made by Stekel: "No one kills himself who did not want to kill another or, at least, wish death to another." This principle of talion, this insight, now so widely accepted in psychoanalysis and so basic to our understanding of the interplay that exists between the murderous impulses and the suicidal drives, could not be understood until much later. Not until Freud formulated his theory of sadism in *Mourning and Melancholia,* could the vicissitudes of aggression be fully recognized. In the light of the new dynamics, the sociological and criminological findings of the nineteenth century assumed relevance and meaning. Only then did the inverse relationship that existed between the rates of capital crime and suicide, and which allegedly were derived from a common "source" (Morselli and Ferri), become more understand-

11 We have often wondered whether this daring pronouncement was not a direct outgrowth of Voltaire's influence on Sadger. For it is reminiscent of the passage in *Candide* in which LaVielle, daughter of Urban X, relates her astounding misadventures to Candide and Cunegonde: "Only a love of life, that still persisted, kept me from suicide."

able. This common source which, at that time, was ascribed to the "decay of the organism" or "degeneracy" is nothing but the interplay of the aggressive and sadistic impulses. This also holds true for many other phenomena. For instance, sociological studies indicated long ago that the suicide rate decreases sharply in times of war and, conversely, increases considerably in periods of social disorganization following wars and political upheavals. We now know that the focusing of aggressive feelings on the enemy cannot be considered the only factor involved in this inversion.

It is perhaps appropriate to remind ourselves at this juncture that Freud's participation in the Symposium was confined to a few general remarks.[12] The "valuable material" apparently

[12] In the light of Freud's early writings one is particularly struck by his reticence at this Symposium. Most impressive to my mind was his observation on the unconscious conflicts generating suicidal impulses as reported in the *Psychopathology of Everyday Life*. I refer to Freud's discussion of the riding officer who became depressed following his mother's death, and who suffered a fatal accident shortly thereafter. The mechanisms of grief, guilt and identification are clearly evident here, an incisive preview of all those elements which he was to expand upon later. In the Dora case, and more explicitly in "The Psychogenesis of a Case of Homosexuality in a Woman" (1920), he expanded further the mechanism of identification. Thus, among the many conjectures and speculations arising from Freud's great caution throughout the Symposium, the most justifiable seems to be that he chose to postpone his theoretical formulation re-

[23]

was not backed up by sufficient clinical evidence to make it conclusive. With the scientific thoroughness and patience so characteristic of him (as reported by Jones, Nunberg, and others), Freud deferred judgment until 1917, when he published his monumental work on grief and pathological depression. He came to the conclusion that "It is this sadism alone that solves the riddle of the tendency to suicide which makes melancholia so interesting—and so dangerous. . . . We have long known, it is true, that no neurotic harbours thoughts of suicide which he has not turned back upon himself from murderous impulses against others, but we have never been able to explain what interplay of forces can carry such a purpose through to execution."[13]

In conclusion, what makes this presentation so meaningful today—apart from its enduring

---

garding suicide only to await clinical validation to bear out his earlier intuitive recognition of the underlying dynamics.

This is not the place to report on the lasting contributions made by many psychoanalytic writers on the problems of suicide subsequent to Freud's formulations. We now know that the displacement of aggression may play a greater role in some cases than in others, and the suicidal act itself is usually overdetermined. Unfortunately, psychoanalytic findings on suicide reached a standstill in the past quarter-century. In the United States, the work of Menninger, Zilboorg, and others will remain abidingly useful, but there is a great need for new clinical research.

13 S. Freud (1917), Mourning and Melancholia. *Standard Edition*, 14:252. London: Hogarth Press, 1957.

scientific value—is the significant role in which the educator cast himself in 1910. He is the one who, standing in the forefront and beckoning the way, challenged the behavioral scientists. Here the teacher assigned to himself the historical role of a psychoanalytic catalyst in the process of linking school and home.

Professor Oppenheim could stand before us today, pleading as he did then for exoneration and vehemently refuting all accusations against the educational system, stressing the fact that suicide in youth was a social phenomenon which stretched much further back in history than the public grasped. Thus, the teacher of Classics in 1910 turned to the emotional life of the child and to the unconscious for elucidation of causative factors. While his eloquent and moving appeal to the scientists was poignant and courageous, his total negation of any involvement on the part of the school in the child's emotional development went beyond demonstrable experience.

Once again, it remained for Freud to clarify, as he did in this Symposium, the balance of factors wherein the school inevitably constitutes a major influence:

> Do not let us be carried too far, however, by our sympathy with the party which has been unjustly

treated in this instance . . . a secondary school should achieve more than not driving its pupils to suicide. It should give them a desire to live and should offer them support and backing at a time of life at which the conditions of their development compel them to relax their ties with their parental home and their family. It seems to me indisputable that schools fail in this, and in many respects fall short of their duty of providing a substitute for the family and of arousing interest in life in the world outside. . . . The school must never forget that it has to deal with immature individuals who cannot be denied a right to linger at certain stages of development and even at certain disagreeable ones. The school must not take on itself the inexorable character of life: it must not seek to be more than a *game* of life. [this volume, pp. 60-61].

PAUL FRIEDMAN, M.D., PH.D.
New York City
February, 1966

Members of the Symposium

PROFESSOR SIGMUND FREUD (1856-1939),
Chairman

ALFRED ADLER, M.D. (1870-1937)
JOSEF K. FRIEDJUNG, M.D. (1871-1946)
KARL MOLITOR, Ph.D. (?)
DAVID ERNST OPPENHEIM (1881-?)
RUDOLF REITLER, M.D. (1865-1917)
J. [ISIDOR] SADGER, M.D. (1867-?)
WILHELM STEKEL, M.D. (1868-1940)

Preface

THE CHIEF aim in publishing these Discussions of the Vienna Psychoanalytic Society[1] is to insure that psychological problems of interest to the community be discussed before a wider circle of medical men, psychologists, and educators from the standpoint of the psychoanalytic method. The Society is well aware of the disadvantages of the form adopted compared with a more unified presentation. The primary disadvantage lies in the fact that conflicting conclusions are presented simultaneously to the reader; the secondary disadvantage is that some aspects of the subject may appear not to have received adequate attention. However, the former probably reflects the varying stages of psychoanalytic practice, while the latter lies essentially in the nature of a verbal discussion and

[1] Translated from *Uber den Selbstmord insbesondere den Schüler-Selbstmord.* Wiesbaden: Verlag J. F. Bergmann, 1910.

[29]

can hardly be corrected by any subsequent
editing of the spoken word. Yet the advantages
of this kind of publication are so obvious that
they justify the decision of the Society to pub-
lish in this way. In particular, it safeguards the
direct connection with the results of psychoanalytic practice, since each speaker necessarily
appeals to his personal experiences. Further,
the anticipation of immediate criticism fosters
a strict discipline of ideas; this is not the case
when writing books. The reader must decide to
what extent the contributors have succeeded in
this respect, and whether the immediacy of the
spoken word is at least in part reflected in the
printed version.

For about seven years, a circle of medical men
and psychologists interested in the study of psychoanalysis have been meeting every week to
discuss their experiences. This circle, which
arose out of the work of Freud and Breuer, is
primarily responsible for the development of
psychoanalytic methods and the advancement
of psychoanalytic experience. Since then, cen-
ters of psychoanalytic study have been formed
all over the world; the number of collaborators,
already quite considerable, is increasing rapidly.
We have every reason to hope that, despite the
desperate efforts of isolated witch-hunters, it

will not be long before we see the majority of the antagonists on our side. On the scientific questions at issue, we do not wish to be judged or tested on the basis of belief or authority; we demand honest criticism and objective scrutiny.

The newness of our science requires some comments about the nature of "the psychoanalytic method." First utilized by Breuer in the treatment of nervous ailments, it was subsequently developed by Freud and his followers. Today, it enables us to illuminate the psychic processes of the healthy and the ill in two directions and to bring their unconscious mechanisms to consciousness: (1) genetically, by laying bare the sources of the psychological end result and tracing the phases of its development; (2) dynamically, by seeking to determine the correlation of the instinctual impulses, be it of instincts acting upon each other, instincts reacting to the tension of the outside world, or the compensatory developments of these instinctual impulses and their disturbances in the psychological superstructure. The therapeutic effect is secured by bringing the individual's unconscious psychological attitudes to the surface of consciousness, where they show themselves in part to have been overtaken by developments or to be exaggerated and capable of correction.

[31]

The psychoanalytic method utilizes the ideas and information provided by the patient in order to break down systematically and to dismantle the psychological end phenomenon, and to construct the simplest disease-inducing situation common to all symptoms. The accuracy of the results can invariably be checked because the presumed pathogenic situation of childhood is always in accordance with the real situation, which is gradually recalled in its entirety. The preconditions for the practice of this method are an accurate knowledge of the child psyche and its development—including that of the sexual drive—as well as the ability to prevent personal ideas from influencing the analysis and to be guided instead by the patient's thoughts and emotional life. In addition, psychoanalysis calls for training and psychological sensitivity.

Whether and to what extent this first discussion offers any evidence of these abilities must be left to the judgment of the reader.

ALFRED ADLER
on behalf of the Vienna
Psychoanalytic Society

Vienna, June 26, 1910

Symposium on Suicide

D. E. OPPENHEIM

It is widely believed that the person best qualified to form a judgment in scientific matters is the one who is least affected by the results of the judgment. He is the only one from whom we expect dispassionate perseverance, objectivity, an absence of prejudice, and all the other virtues of a good judge.

Accordingly, when it comes to the question of the cause and prevention of suicide among students, least attention should be paid to the teacher, even if his own career has never been shadowed by such an unfortunate occurrence. Teachers might be prepared to accept this ruling if it were also applied to those who make a profession of damning our educational system. And yet, each time a schoolchild falls victim to an incomprehensible disdain for life, these people launch fierce attacks on the "murderous" schools, exploiting the eloquence of hatred and

[33]

the power of the daily press. Then, surely, the teacher is entitled to the right of defense.

If the educational system, which is called upon to mould the present and give direction to the future of our society by its quiet but rigorous work, is to be accused, at least it should not wholly lack defenders. Such is the aim of the following remarks; may they not prove wholly ineffective.

If, since it is the negation of the strongest of all human instincts, that of self-preservation, suicide is always anomalous, it is even more so when the suicide takes place in childhood, since we believe that youth combines an undiminished life force with an indestructible will to live.

This intuitive view is fully confirmed by statistical records, which show that the overwhelming majority of suicides are committed after the age of fifteen. Thus, the life-denying children under the age of fifteen who kill themselves constitute a secondary category of deviation from normality. The fact that this category does not increase in the same proportion as the total number of suicides further confirms its peculiarity.

For this reason, an explanation adequate for the suicide of adults may not suffice to make the suicide of children fully comprehensible. But we consider it reasonable to group the cases of child suicide together with suicides committed between the ages of fifteen and twenty and to treat them as one problem, thus extending the investigation of child suicide to an inquiry into the causes of suicide in youthful years.

In public discussion, however, the question, although extended by this grouping, is also drastically narrowed, because attention is concentrated exclusively on those youthful suicides who attend school, and their act is classified as "student suicide." This classification is open to objections, and it does not seem gratuitous to state them as clearly and sharply as possible.

The debate provoked by recent cases of suicide among students shows clearly that the narrow category of "student suicide" is banishing the wider category of "suicide in youthful years" from public awareness, indeed is replacing it, so that little heed is given to suicides among young people who do not attend school. But this does not reveal the full extent of the confusion which is caused by the unfortunate catchphrase, "student suicide."

There are almost eight times as many suicides in the tempestuous period of development between the ages of fifteen and twenty as there are

D. E. OPPENHEIM

in the younger population. In this age group, students are still in the secondary schools, so that "student suicides" are in fact suicides of pupils in secondary schools. This gives a new impetus to the confusion of terms and the veiling of facts. Just as the expression "student suicide" has replaced the more accurate expression "suicide in youthful years," so it is now itself being forgotten in favor of the expression "secondary-school suicide." The latter alone remains in the public mind as a bloody specter, which slaughters with revolting cruelty only those in the flower of youth.

This presentation of the errors that beset our inquiry will be considered exaggerated. But we must recall the discussion that has recently been provoked by the suicide of boys at Viennese secondary schools. Did it not require a statement from the Ministry of Education to remind the public that suicides also take place among apprentices and shop assistants?

The more the suicide of students lets us forget the youthful suicides in other walks of life, the stronger is the demand, implicit in the category itself, that the motive for the deed in every student's suicide be found in his relationship to his school; and the more the school will be burdened with the blame for this sad event.

[36]

It would be easy to demonstrate the deceptiveness of the aura that clings to the expression "student suicide"; to show how often the young suicide's disdain for his life lacks any connection with his school; and how often the connection, on close examination, will turn out to be an excuse rather than the cause. And now, after having discussed some erroneous thinking that confounds the question of suicide, let us examine some relevant historical facts.

Suicide in youthful years is a social phenomenon that stretches much further back in history than our newspaper scribes imagine. It did not await cultivation by secondary-school teachers with autocratic tendencies. Nor should the phenomenon be viewed with the eyes of a provincial newspaper reporter purely as an Austrian or even a Viennese specialty. It is coextensive with the modern world, and has grown with it.

The first evidence of this terrible paradox of suicide in youthful years emerged in the Renaissance, the period that created modern civilization by breaking with the immediate past to return to an earlier epoch. It was a rich period, yet more complex, restless, and contradictory than any that preceded it. One of the first and foremost men of this new age, Michel de Montaigne, chose the phenomenon of suicide in youthful years as the symptom of his day.

By the second half of the eighteenth century, the cases were already so numerous that they demanded statistical registration. In Prussia, statistics relating to suicide in youthful years go back to 1749. The series clearly shows an upward trend. Between 1883 and 1905, the suicide rate for young people rose from 7.02 to 8.26 per 100,000. Fortunately, the figures do not show the same steady rate of increase as the adult suicide rate. There are sharp drops which are leveled out by gradual increases.

Our review of the historical development of suicide in youthful years has shown us something of its geographic spread. We have found it in the France of Montaigne and need hardly add that it still exists in France today. Prussia and the rest of Germany, Britain, Switzerland, and Italy, all keep statistics on suicide in youthful years.

The causes of an evil of such range and antiquity cannot be narrowly defined either temporally or spatially. Therefore, they cannot be ascribed to educational institutions of recent origin that are localized in Austria. But even if we assume that harsh discipline at school is in fact as antagonistic to life impulses as many critics assert, how are we to explain that suicide among the young is increasing although the principle of gentleness toward the weak reigns in all our public institutions, including our schools?

One example will illustrate how much milder school discipline has become in the course of a single generation: when a highly placed and reputable official of our educational service was still a young teacher, he was permitted to mark the work of half a class at the end of the term as "inadequate" or "totally inadequate." Nowadays, no teacher could justify such grading; the mark "totally inadequate" has been abolished, and if the percentage of "inadequate" reaches twenty-five, the authorities will demand an explanation and probably add a stinging rebuke. Even if our schoolboys do not yet lead a free life full of delight, their lot has been eased; and if they still cast it aside more frequently than before, the school cannot be reproached.

But even the increase in the number of student suicides is not beyond doubt. Unfortunately, we have statistical material not for Austrian, but only for Prussian schools. But these are surely not milder than ours; corporal punishment, completely forbidden in our country, is permitted in Prussia up to the top grade of the secondary school. Despite this strict discipline, the number of pupils at all levels who committed suicide was no higher in 1905 than in 1883—fifty-eight for each of these years.

The figures also show no increase in the suicide rate for those Prussian schools that are the equivalent of our own much-belabored secondary schools. In 1883, nineteen pupils of these Prussian schools committed suicide; in 1905, only eighteen.

In 1883, a commission appointed by the Prussian Education Minister, von Gossler, of which Rudolf Virchow[1] was a member, reported that from 1869 to 1881, the statistical material at hand "provided not the slightest evidence for the constantly repeated assertion of an increase in suicide among the pupils of our higher educational institutions." The report indicates why the committee was appointed. It was to review the charges already being made—in Prussia, the land of authority—against the higher schools, because of student suicides. Thus the secondary school has held its ground for almost a generation against the most damaging attack from its enemies; this may encourage its defenders to continue their struggle.

However, while putting forward further evi-

[1] German pathologist (1821–1902).

dence in defense of the much-maligned school, we must simultaneously heed our own warning. The suicide rate for young people in 1905 was 1.26 per cent higher than in 1883. This increase cannot be attributed to student suicides since, as we have just seen, they were not more numerous in 1905 than in 1883. Suicide, therefore, must have increased in that section of youth which no longer attends school but has entered the labor force. It would seem, therefore, that our schools, including our secondary schools, do not encourage the increase of suicide, as is being claimed, but rather inhibit it. Only a thorough statistical investigation could help us form a final judgment on the influence of our secondary schools on suicide trends. Its execution must, of course, be left to the Central Statistical Office; but we might point out the method of approach. There should be a census of all secondary-school students, and one of the same age group in the other walks of life. The annual suicide rate should be calculated separately for these two groups.

The trend suggested by the Prussian statistics leads us to assume that the rate of suicide will be the same in each group, or somewhat lower among secondary-school pupils. It is to be hoped that before long we shall be able to thank the proper authorities for the relevant figures. One fact, however, is already beyond dispute, namely, that our schools are not the only force that drives young people to suicide. This is proved not only by the great number of young people who commit suicide after they have left school; it can also be proved for "student suicides," despite the misleading expression.

The statistics on the rate of suicide among the pupils of Prussian schools take account of the motives. Unfortunately, they fail to distinguish between "harsh treatment by teachers" and "harsh treatment by parents and relatives."

On the basis of a critical examination of the available material, the Prussian psychiatrist Eulenburg[2] was able to trace a possible causal connection between suicide and fear of punishment for some school offense, or humiliation due to academic failure, in only 37 per cent of the cases. In other words, student suicides that warrant the term because they are caused by the schools are very much in the minority.

But the school justifies its existence only as a preparation for life; is not, therefore, every

2 Albert Eulenburg (1840–1917) wrote extensively on the subject of suicide, most particularly of young people. The material referred to here is "Schülerselbstmorde," which appeared in a monthly journal concerned with educational reforms, *Der Säemann* (Vol. 5; Leipzig: Teubner, 1909).

single case in which it causes a flight from life a terrible paradox? Assuredly, but it is precisely the paradoxical lack of proportion between the flimsiness of the motives and the incomparable difficulty of the decision that links these student suicides with those other cases of suicide by young people from which they are usually carefully distinguished.

Because of the fear that precedes it and the humiliation that follows it, a domestic chastisement can just as readily provoke suicide as can punishment in school. And when even to forbid a child to go to the fair, or on an outing with others, is enough to turn some children into suicides, we face a peculiarity of the emotional life of the child that has so far defied all analysis. With this, the riddle of student suicide is swallowed up in the far greater riddle of the psychology and psychopathology of the child. At least some proportion of youthful suicides is pathological. That has been proved beyond doubt for precisely the group we are concerned with here.

Eulenburg's investigation of 320 cases of suicide among Prussia's high-school pupils, based on the detailed official inquiry into each case, showed that 10 per cent of all these youths were clearly of unsound mind. Eulenburg's report adds: "There would probably have been more such cases but for the fact that the official inquiries were often inadequate in this particular respect, which calls for specifically medical evidence" (p. 12).[3]

Among the clearly pathological suicides whose case histories Eulenburg presents in detail (pp. 13ff.), one matriculation candidate, who shot himself in the local cemetery on the day of the written examination, deserves our special attention. How much moral indignation would this sad event yield if it were to be turned against the murderous brutality of the examination system, if one did not know that this unfortunate youth had been in neurological treatment for the previous five years and suffered from a hereditary taint?

This case is instructive for another reason. It forms a link between suicides that follow upon an acute psychological disturbance, and suicides that lack it but show instead "an inborn, more-or-less severe neuropathological strain, a constitutional tendency in the form of inferiority" (p. 15). According to Eulenburg, at least 57 of the 320 cases, or almost 18 per cent, belonged to this second group.

3 See footnote 2, above.

Many of the suicides included in the above number came from alcoholic families, or were burdened in some other way by hereditary taints. Where this psychological abnormality had previously led to one or several suicides by older members of the family, the power of the hereditary predisposition was strengthened by the suggestive force of example. This is a point with which we shall deal later at greater length because of its extraordinary importance. Here, we wish only to stress the inevitability of developmental damage to the child's psyche in an abnormal family.

If a boy is depressed and suffers from feelings of inferiority induced by circumstances such as those we have described, and if he is therefore unable to cope with the demands of his school and does not fight against failure but gives up the struggle and commits suicide, can the school be blamed for his self-destruction?

With the wonderfully keen perception of those at the point of death, once revered with pious naïveté as clairvoyance, one of these unfortunates has answered this question. He was sixteen years old, harshly treated, an illegitimate child going by his mother's name, since his father refused to recognize him even after the relationship with the mother had been regularized. When he failed to be promoted, despite his unrealistic expectations, he shot himself. A visiting card was found in his pocket, on which he had scribbled: "Dear parents, forgive me. I really didn't think it would come to this. My weak character once again makes it impossible for me to bear the disgrace. Give my regards to Dr. E. . . ." Doctor E. was his class teacher. And this unfortunate boy's last words, after confessing to his own weakness of character, were to send him a friendly greeting. Deeply moved, we can only murmur: *Have, anima candida!* ["Oh, honest soul"].

What do we now think of the journalists who present such cases—and there are far too many —in a wondrously simplistic light, unhampered by knowledge of the facts, as student suicides, for which the school is to blame?

But rather than quarrel with those who will not learn, let us seek greater knowledge ourselves.

In almost a quarter of the 320 cases of student suicide for which Eulenburg had adequate data, the germ of the catastrophe lay in the absence of sufficient ability for advanced study (p. 17). So many fall victim to the lack of understanding that makes relatives force young people onto a path which can only lead to failure, however hard they try. And are they not also victims who are forced to spend precious years of their youth in overcrowding the secondary schools, before they are finally allowed to seek escape?

It would be easy to prevent this bitter misfortune of "the far too many" if parents would only pay attention to the warnings of teachers, or give the teachers and psychologically trained school doctors the authority to dismiss pupils who are mentally or physically unfit to pursue further studies. But instead, the embattled advocates of school reform offer a simple and painless remedy. These optimists, who look at the world through rose-colored glasses, are not prepared to promise the one basic reform that would finally settle the matter, the reform of Mother Nature, who still, perversely, creates the untalented side by side with the talented.

But they are not helpless. If the pupils do not suit the school, then the school must be tailored to suit the pupils, until all friction is removed. After all, every tailor knows the trick—why should it elude our wise school reformers? The Stoics taught that the wise man knows all trades. This much-derided paradox now finds an ultramodern confirmation.

Since they have interests outside their schools, our young people will probably go on committing suicide even after this new and comfortable fashion in hats has been introduced. And assuredly the public intellectual life will be victimized. But this is a minor concern. Onward with the slogan, "School reform, and class struggle on behalf of the intellectually inferior!"

But the satiric drama of our school foes must not induce us to forget the very real tragedy of student suicides. Now that we have considered the fatal tension between demands and ability that destroys the life of many good but untalented boys, and leaves a burden of guilt on parents blinded by ambition, let us turn to the equally murderous gulf between youthful demands and obligations.

Its numerous victims—81 out of 320 in Prussia (according to Eulenburg, pp. 17 and 20ff.) are young people of good and sometimes exceptional talent, who, as the result of premature development, seek confirmation of their manliness in both their work and pleasures, but are compelled to lead the life of immature schoolboys. Even the most bitter enemies of our schools can hardly blame them for the destructive precocity of these unfortunates. And who does not recall the famous dunces, from Klopstock[4] to Nietzsche, who were turned out by the schools of their days?

4 Gottleib Frederich Klopstock, German poet (1724–1803).

If our classrooms nowadays are populated by hypermodern poets, ultrarevolutionary politicians, heroic philosophers, and experienced lovers, this reflects the influence of a society that today, as in the formative days of Christianity, once again seeks desperately and painfully to renew its whole life, and most especially involves its youth in this monumental struggle. But why does the school allow its pupils to be wrenched away? Instead of many reasons, let only the simplest serve as justification. Consider what a small part of the year is given to the school for its work with the young. The rest of the time leaves them to the influence of other social forces—primarily the parental home, but also their social life, public opinion, modern art, and literature.

Since even very young people cannot be kept from modern life, would it perhaps be better if the school, the anxious hen, were to follow her chicks into the strange element and splash around in the stream of modernity? Once its protégés were left free to pursue every form of activity as an unvarnished expression of their personalities, where would be the causes of stunted development and perilous conflict?

Such a modern, exemplary school would be quite safe—so safe, in fact, that those lively boys

[49]

who need school rules, if only to break them, would refuse to go near the place. At least this is the considered view of our dedicated teachers, who know young people and still have confidence in them.

But it may be possible to introduce a few prophylactic measures to forestall student suicides without wrecking the traditional educational system. We cannot convince our readers that family life is the decisive factor in the etiology of student suicides, and that academic failure never provides more than the occasion which triggers the catastrophe. This is because we have deliberately restricted the scope of our psychological inquiries to the upper world of the conscious and have not delved into the depths of unconscious thoughts and desires, leaving these to expert practitioners. However, even our superficial inquiries have sufficiently demonstrated the influence of domestic conditions on student suicides to warrant the demand that prophylactic measures begin in the home.

A teacher must observe many children in a relatively short time, and sees primarily their intellectual abilities. He can seldom penetrate deeper layers, if only because these are deliberately kept from him. At home, every child can be observed at length and in his natural attitudes. This permits parents to note the emergence of serious psychological conflicts and to prevent intensification to the point of catastrophe. Unfortunately, such opportunities are not fully exploited. For example, when Eulenburg (p. 14) inquired into the suicide of a nineteen-year-old, he discovered that "this young man had not spoken to his parents and siblings for months and had been left wholly to himself, obviously in a state of deepest melancholy."

What even parents fail to notice will usually also remain hidden from the school. If a teacher is given the necessary clues, he may be able to do a great deal to protect an overstimulated boy from a desperate act. But such fruitful cooperation can be attained only if parents uproot their pathological mistrust and decide to establish a true alliance with the school instead of forging the usual offensive and defensive alliance against it. Perhaps this desirable confidence could be more readily established if the school were to lose the dangerous privilege of passing irrevocable judgments on the performance of its pupils, and a supervisory commission were established to deal with complaints. A pupil who feels that he has been misjudged should be given the right to demonstrate his knowledge before a second examination tribunal. Then even the most vitriolic journalist would be unable to say that in marking a pupil's examination papers "inadequate" a teacher had "signed the boy's death warrant."[5]

From the perspective of a psychology oriented to the deepest layers of unconscious emotional impulses, it is obvious that even our proposed change in the grading system will not remove all causes for suicide among students—that in fact the real and ultimate causes of suicide often cannot be discovered, and are therefore assuredly not prevented by prophylactic measures.

But much could be gained if we tried to make suicide more difficult for the potential candidate. It is true that anyone who is really determined to put an end to his life will find the means to surmount any hindrances that go counter to his intention, and will not hesitate to adopt even the most horrible means of self-destruction. But it cannot be denied that opportunity makes the suicide as well as the thief. An opportunity for self-destruction is offered to anyone who is in the position to bring about his death by some swift and easy action that is painless and avoids revolting mutilations and disfigurement. A loaded pistol complies so well

5 See H. Fischel, "Die Klassifikationssorgen." *Die Zeit*, No. 2790, July 2, 1910.

with all these conditions that its possession positively urges the idea of suicide on its owner, or, as the psychologists say, suggests it. For this very reason, a pupil of our acquaintance who suffered from severe depression gave up a handsome pistol that had been a cherished toy throughout his secondary-school years.

The much-discussed Viennese boy who took advantage of his access to his father's weapon collection to choose the one most suited for his suicide strikes us as the appropriate counterpart to this prudent young man. Of course, without knowledge of the full details, we cannot assert that the very thought of the weapon collection reinforced the emerging decision to commit suicide. But the opposite—the irrelevance of this particular factor—would surely be even more difficult to establish. So we can use this tragic case only to instruct those fathers who heretofore thought that a pistol belongs in the pocket of a real boy no less than a watch.

A pistol produces a suggestive excitation because it embraces the possibility of suicide. The marksman who turns it on himself is subject to even greater suggestion. However, for a full insight into the suggestive force that acts on the suicide, we must remember that among the numerous means for committing suicide, only an actual homicidal weapon, such as a firearm, possesses this suggestive force; rope and matches do not, nor do the river and a top-floor window. But every suicide, no matter how it is carried out, lures others to precise imitation.

Thus, in a certain English town, whose name escapes me, suicides are committed by jumping off a bridge; they take place in a cluster, at intervals of several years.[6] Many similar instances show that suicide is contagious. History records epidemics of suicide even in antiquity. From the end of the fifth century B.C., suicides began to increase noticeably in Athens, at least in part under the influence of the example provided by the real or imagined suicide of the great statesman Themistocles.[7] At that same time, Stheneboia, the heroine of a Euripidean tragedy, was recommending the poison cup to the misunderstood women of Athens (Hirzel, p. 102). In the third and subsequent centuries B.C., the era of Hellenism, the flight from life became a commonplace in Alexandria, then the center of Greek civilization. A pessimistic hedonist, Hegesias, called the preacher of death

[6] A. Baer, "Selbstmord im kindlichen Lebensalter." In *Encyklopedisches Handbuch der Heilpädagogik,* ed. Danneman, Schober, and Schulze. Halle: Carl Marhold, 1911.

[7] R. Hirzel, "Der Selbstmord." *Arch. Religionswiss.,* 1908, p. 91.

(Pesithanatos), had only to discuss the misery of life and the right to self-liberation to move a group of young people to a practical confirmation of his life-denying philosophy. This clearly illustrates how an epidemic of suicide is created by mass suggestion.

In the great center of Hellenistic civilization, imperial Rome, the right to voluntary death was raised to the level of dogma by an opposition that was stoic in questions of ideology and republican in politics.

The irreconcilable enemy of the dictator Caesar, Cato of Utica, who was unwilling to survive the overthrow of the Republic, became the saint and martyr of a community that followed him into death. In addition, certain families had a suicide tradition: for example, a Fannia would take her life because her mother and grandmother, both Arriae, had died voluntarily (Hirzel, p. 104, fn. 1).

In more recent periods of intellectual and moral history, the famous Elizabeth Charlotte, an acute and uninhibited observer of the days of Louis XIV, writes in a letter to the Electress Sophie of Hannover in the year 1698: "It is quite a common thing for the English to kill themselves" (Hirzel, p. 80, fn. 3). Montesquieu adds that it would appear that they did so with-

out any discernible reason (*L'Esprit des Lois,*
after Hirzel, p. 80, fn. 3). The absence of individual motive is a sure indication of suicide
under the influence of mass suggestion. Ham-
let's melancholy soliloquy "To be or not to be"
was well calculated to have such an effect. Then,
in 1668, came *Biothanatos,* a work published in
London in defense of suicide, written, strangely
enough, by an incumbent of St. Paul's.[8]

From the letters of Elizabeth Charlotte, we
can also see that the English contempt for life
spread together with English culture. In 1718,
she writes to the Countess Louise: "Our Ger-
mans are now copying the English habit of kill-
ing themselves, and I really think we could
do without that" (Hirzel, p. 80, fn. 3). In 1722,
she reports to Mr. von Harling: "The great
craze in Paris at the moment is to end one's life"
(Hirzel, p. 83, fn. 4). In Germany, this suicide
epidemic did not reach its peak until the end
of the eighteenth century. This time it was not
a philosopher but a great poet, the young
Goethe, who unintentionally played the role of

8 John Donne (English poet and divine, 1572–1631), *Biothana-*
tos: "a declaration of that paradoxe or thesis that self-homicide
is not so naturally sin, that it may never be otherwise. Wherein
the nature and the extent of all those lawes which seeme to
be violated by this act, are diligently surveyed." London:
Humphrey Moseley, 1644.

the death preacher *(Pesithanatos)*. His Werther's "much-lamented shade" was followed into
the grave by many young men of a similar mind.
And whom was Werther following? Goethe
himself gives us the answer by placing *Emilia
Galotti* on the desk of the suicide (Hirzel, p.
101, fn. 4). And Werther's model, the young
Jerusalem, made famous by his own suicide,
was, surely not by accident, an imitator of the
English during his life (Hirzel, p. 81, fn. 3;
Goethe, vol. 26, pp. 156, 219). His voluntary
end made a profound impression on his friend
Goethe, particularly as Goethe himself already
had come dangerously close to ending his own
life. And Goethe then was under the spell of a
great model, the Roman Emperor Otto, who
stabbed himself when he was defeated by Vitel-
lius in the struggle for the throne (Hirzel, p.
103, fn. 2; Goethe, vol. 26, pp. 221ff.). And so
we see a long chain of suicides, from classical
times to our own day, in which one link carries
the next. The power that forged this chain is
called suggestion.

The lower the powers of resistance at his
command, the less chance will the person have
of escaping it. A child is more open to suggestion than an adult, in suicide as in all other
matters. In fact, the power of suggestion shows

itself with horrifying clarity in many youthful suicides. We will mention only two particularly characteristic cases mentioned in Baer's investigation, "Selbstmords im kindlichen Lebensalter." (See footnote 6.)

Voisin[9] reports that a fourteen-year-old boy hanged himself after having chalked three crosses on a wall and placed a bowl of holy water at his feet. Four weeks previously, this boy's uncle, who was often the worse for drink, had committed suicide after breakfast in exactly the same way. Durand[10] recounts that during the burial of a boy who had hanged himself for an unknown reason, one of the choirboys following the body told his companion that he, too, had decided to end his life by hanging himself. Four days later he carried out this decision.

It is, of course, difficult to counteract the suggestive effect that such suicides might have on children once they have been exposed to them in their immediate environment. Fortunately, it does not often happen that a child comes under such an influence. But nowadays almost all

[9] Hans Rost, in his *Bibliographie der Selbstmord* (1927), lists A. Voisin and Felix Voisin (brothers). Both wrote extensively on problems of suicide around the turn of the nineteenth century.

[10] Max Durand-Fardel, "Etude sur le Suicide chez les Enfants." *Arch. Kulturgeschichte*, 1903.

young people read the newspapers or are present when news items are discussed. Thereby the child repeatedly hears of suicide among contemporaries. It would not be so bad if the newspapers confined themselves to brief reports, but instead the circumstances are elaborated in great detail, and everything is done to stimulate sympathy for the unfortunate victim. In the course of lengthy discussion, the suicide is turned into an innocent murder victim, a hunt for the murderer is instigated, and soon he is found. It is the wicked teacher. His stonehearted cruelty has killed the young hopeful, who has died a martyr in the cause of educational liberty.

Let us now consider the effect of such a press campaign—which is not a product of fantasy but, on the contrary, became a grim reality last winter. Consider its effect on a young person in the most tumultuous period of his development, just when he is beginning to feel himself a man and is searching for a suitable means of gratifying his new-found pride. If he is unable to find such gratification in school, he is shown a way of obtaining it by spiting the school. He takes the hint and picks up his pistol. And so the press, with its noisy campaign against the schools and student suicides, ensures that there will al-

[59]

ways be new victims and no dearth of material for complaints and accusations.

Here rests my defense of the school in the matter of student suicide.

PROFESSOR FREUD *

Gentlemen,—You have all listened with much satisfaction to the plea put forward by an educationalist who will not allow an unjustified charge to be levelled against the institution that is so dear to him. But I know that in any case you were not inclined to give easy credence to the accusation that schools drive their pupils to suicide. Do not let us be carried too far, however, by our sympathy with the party which has been unjustly treated in this instance. Not all the arguments put forward by the opener of the discussion seem to me to hold water. If it is the case that youthful suicide occurs not only among pupils in secondary schools but also among apprentices and others, this fact does not acquit the secondary schools; it must perhaps be interpreted as meaning that as regards its pupils the secondary school takes the place of the traumas with which other adolescents

* James Strachey's translation of Freud's comments in this Symposium is used throughout. *Standard Edition*, 11:231–232.

meet in other walks of life. But a secondary school should achieve more than not driving its pupils to suicide. It should give them a desire to live and should offer them support and backing at a time of life at which the conditions of their development compel them to relax their ties with their parental home and their family. It seems to me indisputable that schools fail in this, and in many respects fall short of their duty of providing a substitute for the family and of arousing interest in life in the world outside. This is not a suitable occasion for a criticism of secondary schools in their present shape; but perhaps I may emphasize a single point. The school must never forget that it has to deal with immature individuals who cannot be denied a right to linger at certain stages of development and even at certain disagreeable ones. The school must not take on itself the inexorable character of life: it must not seek to be more than a *game* of life.

DR. REITLER

Gentlemen, we hardly ever see an adult neurotic in psychoanalytic treatment who has not been troubled by suicidal impulses during his student years. Indeed, it is highly probable that the suicidal fantasies which arise in later life are only repetitions—*mutatis mutandis,* of course—of such youthful suicidal obsessions. I am justified in referring to them as obsessions because these suicidal impulses are undoubtedly obsessive in character. If we wish to make an exact diagnosis, then we must say that we are dealing with a mixed form of psychoneurosis, with a phobia—examination anxiety—complicated by obsessions relating to self-destruction.

Apparently these obsessive suicidal impulses are the direct result of examination anxiety. The patients themselves mention no other cause, and it seems quite plausible to most ordinary people that a young student should torture himself with suicidal ideas because of examination anxiety, and should finally translate them into action.

Up to a point, all this is quite correct—to the extent that it refers to conscious ideas. But this means that it is correct to a minor extent only. Psychoanalytic detection of unconscious associations leads us to quite different and far deeper-lying motives. In particular, the psychoanalysis of all phobic patients shows that, at first, their anxiety was altogether without object—that is to say, that before they feared thieves, fire, crossing the street, examinations, infections, poisons, etc., the patients had gone through a stage in which none of the objects of their fears was present, and they felt nothing but unmotivated anxiety. And this form of anxiety is all the more terrible because it is not anchored in anything real from which the patient can flee, but exists only as a mysterious unknown, a threatening, intangible something in the face of which he is helpless. It is, as some patients well express it, "the terrible fear of fear."

How and when does this primary, objectless fear emerge? According to the results of Professor Freud's investigations, it comes about most frequently when the sexual urge does not find a normal outlet and therefore suffers repression. The unresolved sexual tension changes into anxiety which, since it is probably of a toxic nature, is absolutely immune to psychological influence.

Therefore, when young people suffer from a primary anxiety neurosis, it is usually the result of a sudden attempt to give up masturbation, and to repress the sexual urge. In other words, not masturbation, but the struggle against masturbation, the repression of the libido, leads to anxiety neurosis. But, of course, this toxic anxiety does not long remain independent from the psychological sphere.

Pathogenetic complexes of ideas—more or less unconscious—are probably sufficiently present in any psyche, and particularly in any youthful psyche (especially the onanist complex with all its self-reproaches and feelings of guilt), to yield ample material that can combine with the original objectless anxiety, so that a psychogenetic anxiety hysteria can develop from this primary and probably organotoxic neurosis. This clears the way for the further development of the psychoneurosis.

It is an enormous relief for a patient to be able to find an object that he can fear to replace the groundless anxiety that has made him so helpless. But as this primary object is usually found in the damage from masturbation, the situation, though much improved, is still intolerable. Due to the nature of the object, the anxiety is now intellectually determined, but attains permanence. The previous masturbation cannot be undone and, in the patient's view, the deleterious mental and physical consequences can no longer be evaded—therefore, this constant anxiety without any foreseeable end.

At this point, a further psychological phenomenon arises: the anxiety affect is transferred from the original sexual sphere to a harmless social sphere; in the case at hand, that of young students, it is transferred to the school. A great deal is gained thereby, because the continual anxiety can now be restricted in time. In addition, this transfer to a harmless sphere takes into account the cultural tendency to reduce the emotional affect of the sexual urge as much as possible.

In the present company it is, of course, unnecessary for me to explain either this transfer of the anxiety affect from the sexual sphere to a harmless social one or the psychological mechanism involved in the process. The recognition of this universally demonstrable affect transfer in the lives of both the sick and the healthy is among the most firmly established results of psychoanalytic research.

I should like to point out briefly, in this context, that the transfer of the patient's sexual anxiety to examination anxiety is facilitated first by the fact that the school is the natural immediate anxiety object; the normal anxious anticipation of an examination requires only an intensification from another sphere—in this case, the sexual one—in order to develop into real neurotic anxiety; second—perhaps crucially—because the idea of being subject to examination is intimately tied to the sexual sphere. Psychoanalysts know that the examination anxiety dreams of adult men usually reflect the fear of the psychogenically impotent that they may not be able to pass the sexual "examination" set by the female.

Among students, one often observes anxiety that they will fail to pass their examinations because their intellectual capacities, especially memory, have been damaged by masturbation. In other words, there is a partial return of the anxiety affect, which had been transferred to the examination, to the original masturbation complex.

It is also well known that many children begin to masturbate when their anxiety at school, for example in connection with a written examination, overwhelms them. When the peak of sexual satisfaction is reached, their anxiety disappears. The explanation of this apparently common phenomenon obviously lies in the fact that the anxiety which originally arose from suppressed sexuality has attained an excessive tension for the substituted object, the examination. The original scope has, so to speak, become too narrow; the anxiety bursts its bonds and reverts from the harmless social sphere to its true, sexual sphere. Thus, as soon as the repressed libido is released by the onanistic act, the ensuing relief dispels the anxiety. Such children are not likely to commit suicide. They have found a way to untie their anxiety from the false relationship with the substitute object, the school, and turn it back to its original source, which alone affords relief by lifting the sexual repression. In time, if these boys find the way from infantile masturbation to normal sexual intercourse with women, there is every hope that they will ultimately develop into first-rate, useful adults despite—and perhaps even because of—their previous neurotic anxiety attacks.

But what about the others, those who obstinately fixate their sexual anxiety on the ostensible object, the school, and everything connected with it? They seek, above all, to help themselves in the same way as all phobics, by avoidance of the anxiety-arousing object. The pupil who is afraid of examinations will play truant as often as he can. It would be well if both parents and teachers were to realize that truancy is often not caused by irresponsible vagrancy, but stems more frequently than not from a terrible anxiety that drives the youngster aimlessly through the streets, merely in order to keep far away from the school.

Not all students have sufficient courage for such simple, straightforward truancy. Children who do not dare to wander through the streets during school hours attain their object just as well by staying at home and simulating some illness. It should be noted that such deliberate pretense, if repeated often enough, can result in authentic functional disturbances, which represent a deliberately induced conversion hysteria, later sustained by unconscious compulsion.

The ultimate and most radical means of escaping from examination anxiety is by suicide. If everyone who has been tortured at some time in his life by obsessive suicidal thoughts had actually given way to the impulse, humanity would be decimated, and human civilization destroyed, because the creators of civilization would have killed themselves, and only the great undifferentiated mass of the simple, the insensitive, and the unscrupulous would have survived. Fortunately, the completion of the suicide is the rare exception. For most people, the impulse is sufficient. In fact, the mere idea that the anxiety can be ended once and for all seems to have such a comforting effect that one almost gets the impression that many people are kept alive only by their suicidal fantasies.

DR. FRIEDJUNG

The suicide of a young woman, whose history is well known to me from a reliable source, offers a good illustration of the ultimate motives of the majority of suicides, as these have been discussed here. At the same time, it demonstrates the inadequacy of popular and obvious explanations. As an attractive but no longer young girl, she fell in love with a student who frequented her home. Soon afterward, at the urging of her family, she became engaged to a man who was regarded as a desirable match. However, within a few weeks, she broke off the engagement. She was happy that the young man she loved—who, incidentally, knew nothing about her love for him—defended her against her indignant family. About a year later, she made what seemed like a suitable marriage. But her husband turned out to be impotent, dominated by masochistic tendencies, and unstable. For four years she put up with this unhappy marriage. Although she considered divorce repeatedly, she always allowed herself to be dissuaded by her family. Then, one day, she attempted suicide by taking poison, but was not taken seriously by her family. Meanwhile, the man whom she loved had become a doctor. Throughout this time, he had shown her little attention. Then she had a short period of happiness; a gynecologist diagnosed certain irregularities as indications of pregnancy. The woman believed the practically impossible and looked forward to the birth of her child—until the swelling was revealed as a myoma uteri, which had to be removed by an alaparotomian operation. After her recovery, she discovered that this misfortune frequently happens to childless women. This intensified her dislike for her husband to the point of hatred, because now she blamed him for her mutilation. But a new source of hope arose—now she could approach the man she loved without danger. She began to visit him regularly in his professional capacity, told him of her suffering, and shyly offered herself to him. He remained friendly and detached. One day she told him that she had spent the last weeks with her family, but they insisted that she return to her husband. She had, she said, agreed to return the next day, but wanted him, her best friend, to tell her what she should do. He was in a great hurry, so he spoke a few friendly words and sent her away, implying that at the moment he had no time for her. The woman went to her husband's house and hanged herself. Her family was convinced that she had committed suicide because she was unwilling to take up her unhappy marriage again. Only the doctor realized that she had put an end to her life because he would give her nothing, not even his time.

DR. SADGER

I think that there were two lines of argument in the observations of our opening speaker: first, a general one, in which he stressed the uselessness of all the previous approaches, especially the statistical method. Second, there was a more personal argument, in which he warmly and vigorously defended our secondary-school teachers. He pointed out quite rightly that all commentators, including medical men, completely miss the real point and that they uncritically and credulously restate the most frivolous and superficial motives and do not even seek the decisive factors. As so often happens, the decisive factor here is erotic. I find it particularly astonishing that learned medical men are prepared to accept such specious motives as "passion," "worry," and "vexation," without more precise

[71]

details, while, for example, Baer, who has prepared a series of statistics, was able to find only five cases in one of his categories in which love was the cause of student suicide. The procedure is generally so shallow and unscientific that one is tempted to blame the notorious resistance against any erotic etiology. To discover sexual motives, they must be sought with some determination. Otherwise, they will never be brought to light—not because they do not exist, but because everyone who is questioned likes to suppress them, especially since, thanks to his own repressed eroticism, the investigator himself also does not want to uncover them. Only an investigator who stalks them with determination, instead of consciously or unconsciously overlooking all sexual matters, will find that in most cases of student suicide sexuality is the most fundamental and decisive factor.

Perhaps some of us will recall a similar example from clinical practice. Not so very long ago, diagnosticians would not accept syphilis as the only cause of softening of the brain and spinal tuberculosis, but would present all conceivable alternative diagnoses. Only after recognized authorities repeatedly pointed to luetic infection as the fundamental cause did reluctant diagnosticians increasingly begin to recognize this source. The question then was formulated differently, and, as a result, more reliable results were reached. At one time doctors would ask tentatively, with a show of embarrassment: "I don't wish to be personal, but have you perhaps ever suffered an infection?" to which the patient would almost invariably say, "No." Nowadays a doctor will ask firmly, "When did you contract venereal disease?" and usually get the truth.

When all is well, a man will not usually talk about his love affairs. If the doctor wants to know the truth, he will have to probe, with determination and sympathy; otherwise he will be deceived constantly. There are few things a man will lie about as often and as obstinately as about the expression of his sexual urges. Only a fundamentally honest man of strong character will readily admit to the truth. Generally, one reveals oneself only to someone who shows love. No one can live without love, without sexual activity, least of all during puberty.

When we examine the popularly accepted causes for student suicide, let me exclude those that have been insufficiently investigated. Whoever inquires more closely into vague conceptions such as "passion" and "worry" will often find that it is less a case of ordinary, everyday

[73]

worry than yearning for love and an absence of tenderness in the environment. The same is true of the unknown motives. Now let us consider several causes that must be taken more seriously, such as hereditary taints, insanity, suicidal mania in families, and, finally, suicide by imitation and suggestion. We know that one of the cardinal stigmas of hereditary taint is chronic melancholia, which then usually appears at puberty. But my own analyses have taught me time and again that although the conviction is correct, it is not exhaustive. A little while ago, for example, I described the case of a 32-year-old man from a hereditarily heavily tainted family. Among other things, he suffered from recurring attacks of profound depression, during which suicidal impulses arose. However, psychoanalysis showed that every single attack of depression was triggered by sexual factors. This was true not only in this particular case; repeated experience has taught me that it can be accepted as the rule. In all the cases I have had an opportunity of analyzing I have been able to show that sexual motives were at least the immediate trigger alongside the constitutional factor, although the latter is undeniably an essential condition.

The same is true of the family suicide and

suicide as the result of imitation or suggestion. In recent years, we have found that here, too, there is an inborn inferiority, a constitutional factor. One discovers, for example, that in one family the father shot himself at a certain age; his sons grew up and, at the same age, all turned to the same weapon. In such cases I always suspect a second factor at work, and one which is by no means less significant—namely, an identification with the father, either, as is frequently the case, from great love, or from the same etiological demand that we will deal with later in connection with student suicide. But love, or the unsatisfied need for love, remains fundamental. Even the psychoses yield an illustration. No psychotic commits suicide without some subjectively compelling reason, which we rarely discover. It is not without reason that the suicidal psychosis, melancholia, is an illness of age, of people who observe their declining capacity to love and can no longer hope for love from others. When such melancholics typically complain that, although they are rich, they are impoverished, we know today that it is they who are right, and not the healthy people who, in their arrogant incomprehension, are unable to understand them. It is not money of which they are deprived, but love. At this point I should

[75]

like to formulate a principle on the basis of my own experience: the only person who puts an end to his life is one who has been compelled to give up all hope of love.

Now we should never forget that in addition to love for the opposite sex, which normally comes to mind with the word love, there is also homosexual love, that is to say, love for someone of one's own sex. In everyone, even the most normal, this will often show itself to be stronger than heterosexual love at some period of his life. In order to avoid misunderstanding, let me add that one must distinguish between homosexual inclination and homosexual activity. The former is a universal rule; the latter is the exception and, as a permanent phenomenon, it is confined to the perverse. A homosexual inclination lies at the base of every true, lifelong friendship, every strong sympathy between persons of the same sex. In this common, sublimated form, it plays a tremendous role in everyday life without there being the slightest desire for direct homosexual activity. In fact, people who experience such feelings frequently find true happiness in marriage as well.

But now to turn to our particular subject: student suicide, the great majority of which takes place during puberty. What is peculiar to this period of life? Above all an enormous need for love, although actually it is only later that this need finds its object in the other sex rather than in one's own. This is a point that is almost always overlooked. When we add that this is also the period of sexual enlightenment, with all the emotional upheavals that it arouses in everyone, we bring together the underlying causes for the great majority of student suicides. Most people are at first deeply shocked by sexual knowledge. Quite a few react with complete sexual repression, or exempt their greatest love objects, their own parents. "Others may well be swine, but I don't believe that of my own mother and father," is an indignant denial often heard from boys and girls. Most of them feel betrayed, disappointed in their deepest trust. They can never forgive their parents, particularly the parent of the same sex—because of the deepest homosexual inclination. Now that they have "found out" their parents, the previously existing confidence comes to an end, and the usual casual telling of ordinary happenings ceases. Once their eyes have been opened, the children estrange themselves from their parents. But the need for love is far too strong to be killed, and so despite all resentment, even hatred, affectionate feelings break through.

Then, on some pretext, the child tries time and again to get close, particularly to the parent of the same sex—perhaps because he feels unhappy, perhaps because he sees the future in gloomy colors, etc. Unfortunately, very few parents have sufficient psychological understanding of such outbursts. They take their children's words literally instead of searching for the deeper meaning. And so they try "to talk their children out of it" with reasonable arguments, and may even congratulate themselves on behaving so sensibly. In my experience, they never realize that they have missed the point and have failed to understand and meet their children's need for love. Afterwards, they are astonished when the children they have loved and cherished drift away. What sensible fools they are! At the moment when, as Jung says, "the importance of the father for the fate of the individual" is really decisive, most fathers fail completely.

After this terrible spiritual shipwreck, the boy seeks a new object for his great homosexual need. The nearest such object has long been the teacher, the typical father substitute. But as a rule, the boy suffers even more bitter disappointment here. The majority of our secondary-school teachers know even less about the child's psyche than ordinary elementary-school teachers. The latter know, if they have any insight at all, that every child seeks emotional involvement, has homosexual and heterosexual inclinations. The child blushingly follows the teacher about, whether man or woman; he is delighted if he is allowed to carry the teacher's books home or fetch something that may be required. The child constantly seeks opportunities to show the teacher his love. He will bring small presents to school, sometimes quite ridiculous ones—in short, he behaves exactly like someone in love. Every good teacher knows well that a child will give his best and learn eagerly only if his affection has been won. But our secondary-school teachers are not such good psychologists, although they can certainly object that the adolescent psyche is far less penetrable than that of the child. But here lies their real responsibility for student suicide. Most of them are quite content to give their best instead of eliciting the children's best through their love. I know from my own experience, and it has been confirmed by others, that a pupil learns well only from a teacher for whom he feels sympathy. A teacher whom the child does not like, one with whom there is no rapport, will permanently destroy the child's concern even with an interesting subject. Boys are very sensitive to any evidence of love, and when they blame their teachers' hostility for their poor school work, they are right—not in the usual sense, because the teachers are unjust or unkind, but because the teachers deny their pupils the love without which they cannot work well. "My teacher is down on me" really means, "my teacher does not love me so why should I learn for him."

At this point, the intense sexual need that puberty releases often absorbs all other interests, so that the boy now has neither the time nor the inclination to study. Every secondary-school teacher knows the phenomenon—the boy suddenly fails, or barely manages to keep up. Formerly excellent pupils now have to be passed on sufferance. But our teachers rarely manage to find the explanation in deep-seated erotic tension. I do not deny the existence of, and even know of some born teachers, who are able to talk to such boys with real understanding and, because they are able to give them love, are often able to bring about a very welcome change. Unfortunately, such cases are exceptional, perhaps one in a thousand. Usually, the boy finds neither understanding nor sympathy. When the boy, disappointed in his longing for love elsewhere, must also do without his teacher's affection, it may lead him to complete despair. From this state to suicide on some pretext is then only a short step. A bad report, an imminent failure, or some folly—even the imitation of a suicide with whom the boy identifies by the same etiology, say masturbation—all of these are no more than the trigger and the release. The decisive and all-important factor remains unrequited love. Let me repeat: only the boy who has been compelled to abandon all hope of love throws his life away. This is the point at which a teacher can intervene usefully, but first the bandages have to fall from his own eyes. When our teachers become more loving because they are more understanding, we shall have fewer occasions to mourn a student suicide.

DR. STEKEL

The discussion has shown us how different our opinions are on the subject of suicide. Our colleague Federn,[11] for example, regards suicide as a symptom of health, and he is not alone in this opinion.

There is no dearth of philosophers and poets

11 Paul Federn, Viennese psychoanalyst (1871–1950).

who see suicide as a great and noble idea. Friedrich Theodor Vischer has even composed a proud hymn to "the first suicide." The opening verse runs:

Thee would I know, proud son of God,
Who was the first to spurn in fearful agony
The eternal curse, cowed fear to spite
Turning the sword's point against his breast.

You who first were born to grasp
The raging thought that no man yet had harbored:
The bolt that still as yet struck no man's heart!
To cast away the burden of this life.

Others talk of suicide as "logical." And from the days of classic antiquity we know of many cases in which an individual has decided, as "the sum of knowledge, as the balance of a long and thoughtful life, to seek death without emotion and without pressure, once no more is to be expected and no more can be given to the world." In her book, *Analyse von 200 Selbstmordfällen,* Dr. Stelzner[12] describes this particular kind of suicide as "philosophic." There has even been an attempt to describe the suicide of young Weininger as such a "philosophic" suicide!

12 Helene-Friderike Stelzner, *Analyse von 200 Selbstmordfällen.* Berlin: S. Karger, 1906.

I do not believe in suicide as a voluntary, proud, and redeeming end for a healthy man. I do not believe in logical and philosophic suicides. Who knows what went on behind the scenes? Who knows what personal tragedy was rationalized as *Weltschmerz* and brought a speedy end?

Even if there are such philosophic suicides, they are not of interest to us here. Nor are we discussing the suicide of those unfortunates who really could see no other way out of the labyrinth of pain and distress, conflicts and humiliations, but to flee life. What we are interested in here is a remarkable phenomenon that has already attracted the attention of various psychologists, namely, the increasing number of suicides among young people who, barely grown-up, still half children, suddenly, unexpectedly, and for some apparently trivial reason, put an end to their lives, to the horrified amazement of their environment. Reliable statistics indicate that the majority of suicides among the apparently normal are committed between the ages of fifteen and twenty-five.

What can be the reason for the alarming increase in the suicide rate among young people today? (Recently it has been denied that there is any such increase; statistics is a fine art.) Even

[83]

child suicide, almost unheard of in the past, is increasing from year to year with terrifying regularity. In these cases, are we dealing with normal, healthy individuals whose emotions are so volatile that they are inclined to exaggerate the importance of the moment? Or are those writers correct who regard every suicide as the ultimate expression of an abnormal psychological tendency, of a psychosis that was previously latent and without symptoms? Or is suicide merely the symptom of a neurosis, a "mental disassociation"? Lemâitre[13] is inclined to accept this latter view. By chance, Lemâitre had had an opportunity to examine four people who subsequently committed suicide, and he had noted psychological deviations in each of them. The first was hysterical; the second suffered from various memory disorders; the third showed an *audition colorée;* and the fourth also seemed abnormal.

These instances show how difficult it is to draw the line between sickness and health. If everyone who evinces some abnormality is to be regarded as mentally ill, there would hardly be a normal person left among the educated;

13 Auguste Lemâitre, "A Propos du Suicide des Jeunes Gens." *Arch. Psychol.,* 4, no. 15. The author, a Swiss psychologist (1857–n.d.), was particularly interested in the problem of suicide among young people.

all of us carry a secret fragment of a neurosis (and perhaps even the makings of a psychosis). In a certain sense we all have mental and nervous disorders. There is really no criterion for the mental health of a normal person.

But what do the investigations of Lemâitre, Eulenburg, Gaupp, Baer, and others prove, if they can tell us so little about the inner life of suicides? The observation that X, a suicide, was a neurotic, does not help us much. Only psychoanalysis can provide us with information about the secret motives of a suicide.

No, I think it is the lazy way out to say, in order to relieve our consciences, that all suicides are ill, psychologically inferior persons who are no great loss anyway. The roots of the phenomenon must lie deeper, must be anchored in the particular conditions of our time. What is the shared feature of all cases? Dr. Stelzner writes: "No matter how much we may try to categorize suicides, for example, into the mentally healthy and mentally ill, according to the nature of the psychosis or the triggering cause, there is, with one single exception, a characteristic shared by all: a general diminution of psychological capacity; an inability to use the will, the understanding, or the imagination to conceive of alternatives or a change in the intolerable situ-

[85]

ation, and to use the alternative to tear oneself away from the suicidal obsession. It is not only the superior strength of the obsession, but the failure of all contrary conceptions that plays the decisive role. In somewhat the same sense Goethe puts these words into the mouth of Werther: 'Nature finds no exit from the labyrinth of confused, contradictory forces, and the human being must die.' "

But why does nature find no exit? What secret force destroys all hope and bars all paths for young people, who have their lives before them? How do children reach such hopelessness?

We will never approach an understanding of child suicide unless we first study the psychology of suicide among adults. It is true that in the case of children some other aspects are relevant, but only some. The fundamentals are the same in both kinds of suicide. Suicide is triggered off more easily in children. Their tendency to be emotional, together with a characteristic overvaluation of emotions, means that in similar circumstances, children are more likely to translate the idea of suicide into action. The occasions for suicide are often ridiculously trivial. Their very triviality seems to me evidence that we must seek stronger forces behind the

[86]

triggering impulse. A superficial investigation will not reveal these forces, but they are in some measure accessible to the psychoanalyst.

For a while, every educated European thought it proper to attack the schools and blame them for student suicides. The cases that I have had occasion to analyze have convinced me that the school is only the triggering factor. I want to stress that fear of punishment, unkind treatment on the part of a teacher, or unsatisfactory progress at school are assuredly not the sole causes of suicide.

What is true of the suicide of adults is also true of suicide among children: the suicide is a punishment imposed on himself by the person who takes his life. I am inclined to feel that the principle of talion plays the decisive role here. *No one kills himself who has never wanted to kill another, or at least wished the death of another.* We psychoanalysts know how powerful a role this flirtation with the idea of death, of the nearest relatives as well as of more distant persons, plays in the development of a neurosis. We see almost daily that the patient's deep sense of guilt about his criminal tendencies vehemently demands punishment. Time and again, we find that the neurosis itself, together with the pleasure it affords (which expresses itself

[87]

in a tendency of flight into sickness), also represents the punishment to which the neurotic has condemned himself for his sinful wishes and fantasies.

Death plays an even bigger role in the waking fantasies and dreams of children than in those of adults. Expressions such as "Daddy, when you die I'm going to marry Mommy" or "Uncle, when you die I'll have your stick with the silver knob" are everyday phenomena. We must also remember that punishment of children arouses feelings of hatred and revenge in them that cannot be abreacted and therefore seek a discharge. Such ideas of hate often culminate in death wishes that appear openly at first; later, they appear surreptitiously in disguise; then are repressed, and give rise to neurotic symptoms. It is very common for children to wish an unpopular teacher dead; or at least they would like to see him ill in bed. Often, a far more important figure hides behind the threatening presence of the teacher—the father. And when religious factors, which we shall discuss later, begin to operate and induce inhibitions and stresses, the psychological conflict is complete. The secret court of the unconscious follows the principle of talion—"an eye for an eye, a tooth for a tooth"; it declares itself guilty of the death wish and condemns itself to death. Thus the act of suicide appears as the culmination of a complicated endopsychological process. It is the last scene of the last act of a slowly unrolling psychological drama.

But psychological phenomena are not so simply determined. Punishment for one's own offenses is coupled with a desire for severe punishment of the parents and the teacher: "You will see where your hardheartedness, your lack of love, has driven me." In the course of his childhood illnesses, the child notices that the behavior of his parents changes completely if they fear his life is in danger. The child now wants to rob his parents of their greatest, most treasured possession: his own life. The child knows that he will thereby inflict the greatest pain. Thus the punishment the child imposes upon himself is simultaneously the punishment he imposes on the instigators of his sufferings.

The influence of religion has been mentioned in our discussion. It was suggested that the childish idea of the pleasures that await us in heaven encourages suicide. Statistics do not support this suggestion. On the contrary, in the Latin countries in which faith is firmly rooted, suicide is comparatively rare. For example, from 1891 to 1893 the suicide rate in Germany was

[89]

212 per million inhabitants, in France, 225, and in Denmark, 240, whereas in deeply religious England it was only 87, in Italy, 56, and in Spain, the stronghold of clericalism, 18. My experience shows that *a deep and authentic religious faith tends to inhibit suicide;* neurosis develops in part from a conflict between faith and unbelief—a conflict that goes back essentially to the struggle between intellect and emotions. Christianity has always tried to repress the tendency to suicide. In this connection a pertinent aphorism of Nietzsche occurs to me: "Christianity turned the tremendous urge to suicide that existed at its inception into a lever of its own power. It allowed only two forms of suicide, and surrounded these with the highest honor and hope, while simultaneously it strictly forbade all others. It allowed only martyrdom and the slow self-destruction of the ascetic."

These observations of the great philosopher adumbrate a second problem—the "chronic suicide." By this I mean the tendency to put an end to one's life not instantaneously by one heroic act, but by a series of deprivations. This latter form is by no means uncommon among children. Consider the hysterical refusal to eat, the complete lack of appetite culminating in disgust at any nourishment (though this certainly has other causes as well). Consider, too, the indifference with which some children will deliberately expose themselves to chills and infections. This "chronic" form of suicide must be taken into account in any psychological investigation of the problem. One particular form of chronic suicide deserves a separate discussion. I am referring to masturbation. It is not widely realized that masturbation is also practiced as a punishment and a penance, as a means of shortening life. The connection between pleasure and punishment is not unknown to us. We need only to recall flagellantism and the ascetic practices of eccentric holy men. Later on we shall see what a tremendous role masturbation plays in the creation of a suicide. At this point I wish to stress that the threats used by parents in the hope of ending their children's masturbation—often prophesying the most terrible consequences for health and well-being if the vice is continued—frequently have the contrary effect. Some obstinate children continue to masturbate precisely in order to shorten their lives. They pay for their secret pleasure by supposing that they are sacrificing a part of their vital force. The forbidden and titillating flirtation with death enhances the pleasure.

Before I deal with the significance of masturbation in suicide, I would like to report the curious observation that suicide is much more common in small families than in large ones. I have observed repeatedly that it is the only son or the only daughter who commits suicide. There is food for thought here. We have long realized that in seeking the reasons for the rapid increase of neurosis we must take families with one or two children into account. Of necessity, the exaggerated tenderness in a family with two children must increase the number of child suicides. Where there are few children, their ambitions are recklessly inflamed. The parents expect the child to fulfill all the far-reaching plans they themselves could not realize. The child must be the first in school, ahead of all the others, become someone outstanding, a great artist, etc. So long as the child can indulge in these ambitious dreams, they add to the joy of life. But one day the fine plans come to nothing, and the house of cards collapses. The adolescent realizes that he cannot "reach the top," and he has not the moderation to be content with the possible. Thus a new motive develops to reject a life that does not fulfill his secret wishes. The initial acceptance of the parents' overvaluation opens a consequential path to the child's own undervaluation.

Dr. Sadger was quite right when he said that people take their own lives only when they can no longer expect love. But this formulation requires extension and development. There are people who have lost the courage to love, who have been robbed of the enjoyment of love by inhibitions, parental injunctions, and social pressure, who are unable to experience libido without guilt. I recall the case of a girl, filled with an ardent desire to love, instinctually driven toward sexual expression, but so surrounded by strictures and inhibitions as the result of an ultramoralistic upbringing that in the end she could see no alternative but to take her own life. Her fear of love was as great as her desire for love. She was too weak to follow her sexual drive, too moral, too burdened with trite middle-class morality. On the other hand, a life without sexual fulfillment was not worth living, and so she decided to resolve the irresolvable conflict by taking her life.

This case also reinforces Professor Freud's contention that suicide often involves incestuous ideas, which are the source of the profoundest guilt feelings. This girl had experienced an incestuous trauma in her childhood, with her brother as its object. Perhaps her inability to love went back to this experience. She was too firmly attached to her family. Apart from moral inhibitions, there was this secret bond which linked her to her brother. She knew only one true love—that for her brother, who was her first love, the love that she could never forget. To escape from this dilemma she chose the solution of suicide. But another aspect is involved in an analysis of her case—an aspect that I have never failed to observe in any of the cases of suicide, or of suicidal intentions, I have had an opportunity of analyzing: the suicidal ideas arose in this patient only after she had given up masturbation. Her strict abstinence from masturbation was one of the causes of her suicide. We realize today that for such people masturbation is of great importance; it cannot be replaced even by the sexual act itself, because it is tinged with partly conscious, partly unconscious incestuous fantasies. The self-reproaches of such patients about their masturbation are in reality directed against these incestuous fantasies. And so it was in this case, too. The patient unconsciously linked her experience with her brother and her autoeroticism. The renunciation of masturbation also required the renunciation of these incestuous fantasies. Her suicide—which was, fortunately, not successful—took place after she had left her parents' house and found a position abroad. To end her life, she took a mixture of morphine and veronal, which she immediately threw up (disgust, as with the sexual act!). This chosen type of suicide, by poison, was also determined by her fantasies, in which the idea of pregnancy played a dominant role.

Another patient experienced the suicidal impulse only some months after having given up masturbation. The urge to "do violence to herself" became more and more powerful. The very expression reveals suicide to be a symbolic substitute for the autoerotic act. Let me recall the words of the philosopher-poet Vischer, who called the first suicide "proud son of God." This is reminiscent of the pride of the autoeroticist who professes that he can do without the world and be sufficient unto himself. The patient of whom I am now speaking, the wife of a doctor, had masturbated from her earliest years; after marriage she found herself sexually frigid. Only the continued masturbation provided sufficient libidinal gratification to keep her in good health. One day she read an article in an encyclopedia about masturbation which frightened her so deeply that she began to abstain. This abstinence caused a severe neurosis that nearly developed into a psychosis with suicidal impulses. The analysis made it clear

[95]

that the threatened suicide actually represented the ultimate autoerotic act.

Another case strikes me as even more convincing. It is that of an elderly artist who decided to end his life. He obtained what he thought was a dose of potassium cyanide from a friend and drank it in the firm belief that he was committing suicide. In fact, it was only a dose of potassium bromide, and the deceived man woke up after a deep sleep with nothing more serious than a headache. This patient also suffered from obsessive ideas and suicidal impulses, as well as self-reproach about masturbation, which he had continued well into old age. His most serious obsessional idea was that someone would come up and attack him. This was actually a homosexual reminiscence dating back to his ninth year. The anxiety here reflected a burning desire to find the satisfaction that had yielded the highest libido, because pleasure was also derived from homosexual impulses. This same patient also had a serious incest trauma in his past (with his sister). In his case, also, the abandonment of masturbation coupled with a profound sense of guilt proved to be the mainspring of the suicidal impulses. The fear that someone might come up and attack him stemmed from the wish that his sister would approach him. His dearest wish had thus become his deepest anxiety.

I would also like to report the case of a fourth patient, who masturbated until his thirty-fourth year. Once again the suicidal impulses arose with the abandonment of this autoerotic satisfaction. In this case, too, the analysis clearly showed that the autoerotic act was coupled with incestuous fantasies. In his childhood he had suffered from bladder trouble. The hand of his mother gently stroking his penis was sufficient to relieve the difficulty. He imitated this procedure in masturbation. Every form of onanism is, of course, a return to an infantile form of sexual satisfaction, a return to the original sources of pleasure. This patient's potency was also unreliable, and sometimes he could obtain an erection only as the result of this same process. An additional factor has to be taken into account in this as in all other cases: namely, that in all onanistic acts (see case three) we are faced with a compromise between homosexual and heterosexual impulses. In this case in particular it was quite clear that masturbation represented a homosexual act as well as an incestuous fantasy.

In all these cases the patients were incapable of enduring a life without masturbation. For them masturbation was not the punishment and penance I mentioned earlier, but a secret pleasure to which a deep sense of guilt was attached. Such guilt, as the observations of other doctors also indicate, can become so intense that suicide is committed immediately after an onanistic act. Here disgust plays a large role alongside masturbation. Such autoeroticists regard their autosatisfaction as a "disgusting" and degrading act. The disgust with themselves turns into disgust with life and with the whole world. Life measured only in terms of sexual gratification loses its value. It is dominated by the affect of rejection. Thus masturbation in its repressed forms also leads to suicide. In particular, onanists who have managed to abstain from onanism for some time, and have succeeded in a struggle against it, may kill themselves after a relapse that robs them of their proud hopes of recovery. With their last onanistic act, i.e., their suicide, they impose the final supreme punishment on themselves.

I wish to mention the analysis of a boy suffering from suicidal ideas, whose case history I described.[14] In my book *Nervöse Angstzustände*[15]

14 Zwangszustände, ihre psychischen Wurzeln und ihre Heilung. *Med. Clin.*, 6:169–172, 213–215, 254–256.
15 Vienna and Berlin: Urban & Schwarzenberg, 1908.

I pointed to the psychological roots of stammering. A boy who suffered in this way and whom I treated last year told me that he did not stammer when he put his hand to his nose. If he pressed the bridge of his nose with his right forefinger, he could immediately speak clearly and fluently. This boy was a persistent onanist, and his secret anxiety was that people might realize that he masturbated. His father had once told him that he should sleep with his hands outside the bedclothes, which suggested to the boy that the father feared that his son might masturbate. Now what was the significance of this symbolic action? With his hand in his pocket, he could still masturbate, but if he put his hand to his nose he demonstrated to the whole world that he was not masturbating. "Look! I don't have my hand in my pocket. It's on my nose." Here his nose was a symbol for his penis, and by this obsessional action, he revealed as much of his secret to the informed as he wished to conceal. This same boy also suffered for a time from obsessional lying. One day he told me a long story that I immediately recognized as a lie. I asked him at once why he was lying to me. He defended himself by saying that he couldn't help it—it just "came over him" and he had to lie. The previous day, it appeared, he had also lied to his father without any necessity at all. His teacher had suddenly fallen ill, so his class was sent home for the rest of the day. But when he arrived home, he told his father that they had been sent home because the roof needed repairing. He was unable to give any reason for this pointless lie. Had he been pleased to have a day off from school? Yes, he had, very much.

"So that really means that you were glad that your teacher had fallen ill, instead of feeling sorry for him, as a good boy should." This, he admitted. He had often wished that his teacher would fall ill, but he hadn't liked to reveal this ignoble feeling to his father. But he had also wished that his father would fall ill—as was brought to light by the analysis. This is more fundamental than the previous conflicts, and I trust you will spare me the necessity of pointing up the motive for this wish. However, this was only one of the motives for this lie. Another was that he wanted to "test" his father. He wanted to find out whether his father really "knew everything," and particularly whether his father could recognize that he masturbated and that he concealed "wicked ideas" in his mind.

A little earlier this boy had had a disagreeable experience. He was being treated for his stammering by a specialist, who had read in my book that stammering was connected with masturbation and repressed sexual desires. After this boy had been sent to him for treatment, and he was alone with him, he tested his reflexes, then looked at him questioningly and said: "You masturbate." This was, of course, the worst thing he could have done, because the boy was suffering from anxiety that everyone would notice that he was a masturbator. Indeed, it was precisely on account of this anxiety that he stammered—not only in general company, but even in the presence of his mother and father, whereas when he was alone he could, like all stammerers, speak fluently. Now this specialist confirmed his fear that people would recognize his secret "vice" at a glance. Thereafter, he tried to demonstrate to the whole world, by his obsessional action of placing his hand on his nose, that he was not masturbating. I learned all this from him. Now why had he lied to me? Just as he wanted to destroy the idea of his father's omniscience by his lie to him, now he lied to me in order to "test" me, and find out for himself whether I really could discover "everything" about him, because I had already told him a great deal about his inner life that no one else had ever guessed before. This lying took place out of unconscious "repressed" motives and was therefore obsessional in character.

In this case we can see the whole secret mechanism at work: the sense of guilt toward father and teacher whose deaths he had wished, and the inhibitions that burdened him. We can see that suicidal impulses necessarily arose because of his inability to give up masturbation. There were days when he felt terribly tired and longed for peace—days on which it would have needed but little encouragement to persuade him to put the omnipresent fantasy of suicide into action. As it happened, he was first in his class; how would it have been if he had been last?

I cannot resist, finally, telling you about a very recent experience dealing with the analysis of a schoolboy suicide, because it strikes me as eminently suited to prove the opinions that have been expressed here.

It concerns an eighteen-year-old commercial student, who went off to school in the morning, followed the lesson with close attention, and an hour later put a bullet in his head. On the face of it, the cause for his suicide was obvious—unrequited love. A couple of months previously he had formed a relationship with a young girl and had told his parents that he wished to become engaged to her. His parents refused their permission for the engagement. According to his first statement, he had tried to take his life because he felt he could not live without the approval of his parents. After several weeks in the hospital, he recovered completely and was able to resume his studies. His parents, who had been deeply shocked by his action, now gave their consent to his engagement; but while he was in the hospital he had discovered that he no longer loved the girl, and so after some months it was easy, and not a sacrifice, to break off the relationship.

He now admits that revenge fantasies directed against his parents were decisive in his suicide attempt. He had looked upon himself as a lost soul who could no longer think and who was faced with madness.[16] All his life he had felt a great need for affection, and this had been given him by an older sister. We learn that when they sent him their letter of refusal, the parents had also enclosed a letter from this sister in which she, too, opposed the engage-

16 The fear of madness plays a large role in suicide. It results from the unconscious psychological conflicts already described—guilt about masturbation and incestuous fantasies. They strive to force their way into consciousness, but are repressed with all available energy.

[103]

ment and insisted on the hopelessness of his love. It was shortly after receiving this letter that he attempted suicide.

A preliminary examination of his sex life showed no particularly striking variations from the normal. Led astray by contemporaries at the age of fifteen, he had gone to a prostitute, but had been completely impotent. In his final years at school he had begun to masturbate, and had experienced a heretofore unknown pleasure. However, he had read a number of books which insisted on the deleterious nature of masturbation, so that he abandoned the practice for fear of shortening his life. Now and again, after this, he had sexual intercourse with prostitutes and servant girls. In his last year at school he masturbated only three times. *He admitted, however, that the libidinal satisfaction achieved during the normal act was never so great as that which he achieved by masturbation.* We now learn that his masturbation was actually coupled with incestuous fantasies. During his first act of masturbation, he had suddenly wondered whether he could perhaps possess an older woman, when, to his horror, his mother appeared before his eyes. We can now understand why he gave up masturbation. His morality prevented him from continuing to seek this kind of satisfaction. He now remembered various events that confirmed the existence of an incestuous inclination toward his mother. Once, during a trip in the mountains, he had met an ugly old peasant woman, and "wicked ideas" had come into his mind, which, full of disgust, he had suppressed. Various of his dreams concerned his mother and his sister. His relationship with the girl to whom he had wished to become engaged had been a very intimate one and would probably have led to the ultimate consequences but for the fact that he felt an inhibiting force, which prevented him from having sexual relations with his beloved although she invited him to do so. *He treated her like a sister.* He also confessed that he had carried out various pederastic acts with a younger brother.

Anyone well-versed in psychoanalysis can see at once that the attempt at suicide was a case of *poena talionis.* Letters from his sister and his mother speaking of the hopelessness of his love affair tipped the balance. An identification was brought about between his girl friend and his sister—who had the same Christian name—and this identification made the hopelessness of all his incestuous fantasies quite clear to him. He transferred the conflict from the mother, the sister, and the brother to the beloved, whom he had treated "as a sister." What then was the cause of his suicide? Not the letter of refusal from his parents, and not the hopelessness of his love for the girl, whom he could have possessed. *No, it was only his deep sense of guilt: the insolubility of his inner conflicts, and his inability to continue masturbation as a substitute for incestuous fantasies and homosexual acts.*

We also learn that his first act of masturbation followed immediately upon a visit to a prostitute—a successful visit this, be it noted. This proves to us that the reality could not give him the same satisfaction as the autoerotic action coupled with incestuous fantasies. This example yields another insight. From earliest childhood, he had been given to frightening his parents. On one occasion, he had locked himself in his room and scratched his hand, wishing to frighten them with this childish pretense at suicide and bend them to his capricious wishes. We note that the suicidal tendencies reach far back into his childhood years. This confirms our psychoanalytic experience, which teaches us that the first years of childhood establish the rhythm that determines the adult fate.

In my opinion, therefore, the deep-rooted

causes of child suicide are to be found in a defective upbringing that overwhelms the child with exaggerated fondness, luring him into incestuous fantasies. The child, who has been so aroused that he cannot live without libidinal satisfaction, is burdened with such tensions that he is incapable of experiencing pleasure without a sense of guilt. I think I have shown that the horrors attributed to the act of masturbation—itself harmless, in my opinion—contribute heavily to the increase of child suicide. It is the hygienic, moral, religious, and ethical inhibitions that make both the child and the adult incapable of enduring life.

This is the point at which we should intervene. It would offer teachers a rewarding task, and make them true teachers of mankind: I am saying, of course, that *the school is not responsible for the suicide of its pupils, but it also does not prevent these suicides. This is its only, but perhaps the greatest, sin.* The school should help its pupils in that period when their sand castles collapse and life brutally shows them the impossibility of realizing their fantasies. *The child and the neurotic perish from the irreality of their fantasies.* The fact that there are so many gifted children who abandon everything life has to offer them because they pathologically exaggerate a fugitive emotion merely proves to us that we have not understood how to prepare our children in time for this collapse of their ideals, that our teachers have failed to guide their pupils from the world of the fairy tale into that of life. Our teachers have failed to give our adolescent youth the horizon that their own psychological narrowness of outlook makes impossible. They have failed to convince the child of the triviality of personal experiences compared with the limitless abundance and infinity of life itself.

Education is the preparation of the child for adult life. We persuade ourselves that if we give the child "a beautiful childhood" we give him a store of memories rich enough to last him the rest of his life. We forget that an ear made sensitive to pure harmonies can be all the more grievously upset by any sudden disharmony, and that the finest effects can be secured by dissolving disharmonious chords. Every educator who encourages a child to forego a pleasure is on a higher ethical plane than one who leads him from pleasure to pleasure.

The school should seek to lead the child gently, so to speak, playfully, from the realm of fantasy into real life—not with empty formulas, accusatives and infinitives, algebraic lumber, and confusing masses of dates; not with harsh examinations and torturous grammar. It should know how to awaken the child's senses to the riches of life and nature, the imperishable masterpieces of ancient and modern art, and, indeed, all the achievements of human civilization. We cannot yet estimate what a tremendous role the greatest teacher of humanity—history —could play in this process. In sum, a child should be able to find that love in school which he is used to, for which he longs, and which he finds so lacking. A child should be given the opportunity to sublimate his sexuality and convert surplus energy. The teacher should be a friend to his pupils, and himself be a student of life. His most earnest endeavor and his proudest aim should be to break through the old imperatives, to present new aims, and to create free and independent human beings.

DR. ADLER

The value of statistical data should certainly not be denied so long as they provide us with a picture of the incidence of suicide and its particular circumstances. However, it is impossible to draw conclusions on the basis of statistics alone about the psychological particulars or the reasons for suicide. So long as the driving forces remain unknown, one will be all too ready to accuse institutions or individuals. Social privation, inadequate school equipment, errors in the educational system, and many other weak points in our civilization may be revealed in the process.

But does any of this clarify the psychological situation of the suicide, the dynamic force that drives him out of life? When we learn that the most densely populated parts of the world have the highest incidence of suicide, and that suicides cluster in certain months of the year, do we thereby learn a single adequate, explanatory motive? No, we learn only that the phenomenon of suicide is also subject to the law of great numbers, and that it is related to other social phenomena. Suicide can be understood only individually, even if it has social preconditions and social consequences.

This recalls the development of neurosis theory, and reminds us that as long as we are not fully clear about the psychological circumstances of the suicide and about the nature of its motives, we are nowhere near an understanding of the problem or a fundamental cure.

Even if we found social techniques to prevent individual suicides, such as the Salvation Army attempts in London by inviting prospective suicides to come to them for consolation and assistance, even if it were possible to reduce the number of suicides materially by deeper religious faith, improved education, social reform, and social assistance, it would, nevertheless, remain worthwhile to clarify the psychological mechanism and the mental dynamics of suicide. First, it might create the possibility of both an individual and social prophylaxis through educational measures and social reforms. Second, because the psychological make-up of the suicide is obviously related to other psychological states and attitudes, particularly those of nervous and psychological sickness, the development of such an integrated view in connection with one problem could be used to further our understanding of others.

This attempt to arrive at a more integrated view is materially supported by popular opinion, which always tends to grant the suicide the extenuating circumstance that he was not responsible for his actions; it is also fostered by psychiatric research into the connection between insanity and suicide.

What material will provide a neurologist who uses the psychoanalytic method with information that will help him to solve the problem of suicide?

The successful suicide thwarts direct insight, for example through questions or reaction tests. In such cases all that remains is documentation and the testimony of the environment, which must be accepted with reserve and is significant only if it is in accord with basic psychological knowledge. Especially with regard to the evidence of those who knew the victim, we must always remember that the excessively sensitive nature of the suicide is always disguised and wrapped in secrecy.

What remains for investigation by the psychoanalytic method are, therefore, the unsuccessful suicide attempts, and the very frequent abortive suicidal impulses. Here the problem is complicated by the fact that such cases are ambiguous because they are ridden by doubt. They choose unsuitable means, seeking death and rescue simultaneously.

Yet this is the only way to obtain certainty about the kind of people who seek death and about the motives that impel them. And here I can say with complete confidence that the decision to commit suicide is arrived at under the same conditions that produce a nervous ailment (neurasthenia, fear and obsessional neurosis, hysteria, and paranoia) or an isolated attack. I have described this "neurotic dynamic" in a number of works[17] that are to be regarded as continuations of my book *Studie über Minderwertigkeit von Organen*.[18] The main ideas developed in these books are as follows:

Every child grows up in circumstances that force him into a dual role, without his being consciously aware of this. He does, however, know it emotionally. As a small, weak, and dependent being he feels a need for support, tenderness, and assistance. Before long he bows to the force that makes it the duty of the weaker to obey, if he wants to satisfy his instinctive needs and win the love of his caretakers. All related traits in the adult, such as submissiveness, humility, religious belief, and belief in authority (suggestibility, the capacity to be hypnotized, and masochism in nervous people) develop from this original feeling of weakness, and they represent psychological patterns that are obviously already marked by traces of aggression, efforts to obtain love and derive gratification from the environment.

In the course of development, there gradu-

17 "Über neurotische Disposition." *Jahrb. Psychoanal. Psychopath. Forsch.*, 1:526–545, 1909; "Psychischer Hermaphroditismus im Leben und in der Neurose." *Fortschr. Med.*, 16. Leipzig: Thieme, 1910.

18 *Study of Organ Inferiority and Its Psychical Compensation* (1907). New York: Nerv. Ment. Dis. Publ., 1917.

ally appear such features as willfulness, a striving for independence, defiance, and even megalomania, which increasingly come into conflict with obedience. One soon observes that, under environmental pressures, this conflict steadily increases as the childish ambition to become big and satisfy his urges (for example, the urge to eat, the urge to display, etc.) develops. The roots of this conflict of character traits lie in the innate contradiction between submission and the urge to satisfy drive impulses. The child soon notices that even in his own small world the thing that counts is force, and later on finds ample confirmation in the world at large. He therefore retains only those features of obedience that seem to yield a gain in love, praise, tenderness, or reward. Unfortunately, it is just this kind of relation to life that will lead the child astray; from the unconscious, he can tendentiously create situations in which the adult is positively dependent on the help of others. In every sickness, inadequacy, fearfulness, and weakness—at school, in society, and in life—such children will always arrange their relationships in such a way that people will take part, show them sympathy, help them, never leave them on their own, and so on. If they do not succeed in bringing about this state of affairs, they feel insulted, neglected, and perse-cuted. *At the same time an abnormal sensitive-ness insures that their own weakness is never exposed.* It is always fate, bad luck, poor educa-tion, the fault of the parents or of the world in general that is responsible for their troubles. Along these lines, they now exaggerate their already excessive sensitiveness to the point of hypochondria, neurosis, and *Weltschmerz.* In-deed, their longing for sympathy and prefer-ential treatment can become so intense that they learn to value sickness as a means of focus-ing the interest of the environment on them-selves, and *at the same time as an excuse to evade every decision. This fear of decisions (the nervous fear of examinations) that keeps them from ever finishing anything they start, but si-multaneously fills them with the utmost impa-tience, and makes the necessity of waiting (for the decision, for success) sheer torture, is under-standable only when one knows the megalo-manic ideas of the unconscious and the feeling of their unrealizability in specifically nervous persons.*

This intrapsychic tension, the dialectical change from the feeling of weakness in the child to megalomania in the adult, is accompanied, but also preserved, by constant feelings of anx-

[115]

iety, insecurity, and doubts about personal capacity. The tension increases in proportion to the dynamic effect of the contrast, and to the augmented hypertrophic development of ambition and vanity.

By reducing this excessive psychic tension to its beginnings in early childhood, psychoanalytic methods make it possible to explain the reasons for its importance and its exceptional strength and persistence. In all cases that involved nervous and unusually talented men, and would-be suicides, I was able to show that, in early childhood, they had suffered from a particularly deep-seated feeling of inferiority. Many years ago, I laid the blame on an inborn organic and systemic inferiority, which handicapped the child through sickness, weakness, fatness, ugliness, deformity, or such childhood troubles as bed-wetting, evacuation difficulties, speech defects, and impairment of vision or hearing.[19]

The vigorous attempts to overcompensate that result from this feeling of inferiority, the

19 Recently, Bartel of Vienna has drawn the connection between suicide and a particular example of organic inferiority, the lymphatic constitution. In the broader interpretation adopted by this author it will—like the organic inferiority I underline—turn out to be a basis for neurosis. In both cases the key to an understanding of the relationships lies in the original childhood feeling of inferiority.

equivalent of overcoming the defect by strenu-
ous training of the mind, frequently succeed,
but not without leaving permanent traces of
adaptation and of the excessive psychological
effort it required. The onetime bed-wetter can
become a hygiene fanatic and achieve extreme
bladder control; the child who suffered from in-
voluntary fecal discharges can become a hyper-
esthete; an original weakness and sensitiveness
of the eyes occasionally make a man into a poet
or a painter; the stammerer Demosthenes became the greatest orator of Greece.[20] Such people are plagued throughout life by an insatiable appetite for success, and their abiding extreme sensitiveness urges them to attempt to
scale the topmost heights of culture. Vengefulness, pedantry, greed, and envy accompany this
development, side by side with indications of
excessive aggressiveness, and even cruelty and
sadism.

Psychic tension may be increased by one more
pertinent factor—namely, a pathological process
which culminates in antithetical dynamics. It
originates in the frequently encountered phenomenon of psychic hermaphroditism. The
dual role misleads children into drawing an ob-

[20] See also J. Reich, "Kunst und Auge." *Österreich. Wochen-
schr.*, 1908.

vious analogy as the result of a judgment which, though based on facts, is false. It is an analogy to which a great part of humanity has always succumbed and which many outstanding personalities—to mention only Schopenhauer, Nietzsche, Möbius, and Weininger—have sought to sustain with witty sophisms. I am referring to *the identification of the characteristics of submissiveness with femininity, and the characteristics of aggressiveness with masculinity.* This valuation is repeatedly forced on the child by his family relationships and by his environment, so that before long he perceives every form of aggression and activity as masculine and all forms of passivity as feminine. Then the child seeks to abandon obedience for defiance and docility for naughtiness—in short, he develops from the normal childish state of tractability and gentleness to intensified megalomania, obstinacy, hatred, and vengefulness. And in appropriate cases (where there is a strong feeling of inferiority) a vehement masculine protest is provoked both in boys and girls. Even the physical weaknesses and defects of the child will not be despised if they can be made to serve as a weapon to secure the constant interest, and a certain dominance over the environment, be it through sickness, headaches, bed-wetting, etc. *Thus the unconscious creates a situation in which sickness, even death, is desired, partly in order to hurt the relatives, and partly to show them what they have lost in the one they have always slighted.* In my experience, this constellation invariably creates the psychological basis for suicide and suicide attempts; but in later years *it is no longer the parents, but the teacher, or some beloved person, or society, or the world at large, that is taken as the object of this act of revenge.*

I must also mention briefly that one of the most important driving forces behind this masculine protest is the frequently encountered uncertainty and doubt on the part of the child concerning his present or future sexual role. This uncertainty, which leads to the ambivalence, the dualism, the doubt and vacillation of the neurotic, vehemently impels boys and girls to every form of masculine protest. *All forms of early sexuality and autoeroticism come from this vehement striving. Masturbation becomes compulsive, and a ceaseless striving after "manly" sexual activity (including Don Juanism, Messalinaism, perversions, incest, rape, and so on) hardens as a symbol of masculine protest.* Love itself degenerates into an insatiable thirst for triumph; the satisfaction of the sexual urge finds a secondary purpose in the proof of manliness, or, along a psychological sideline *(as in the case of masturbation) as self-inflicted damage for purposes of revenge. With this, however, a further precedent is created for a possible subsequent suicidal constellation*—the sensual pleasure of suicide takes the place of the sensual pleasure of masturbation.[21]

The idea of suicide arises under the same set of circumstances as neurosis, the neurotic attack, or psychosis. Suicide and psychosis, like neurosis, are the results of the same psychological constellation, which is brought about in the cases of those so disposed by a disappointment or a humiliation which rekindles the feeling of inferiority from the days of childhood. Both suicide and neurosis are attempts of the overburdened psyche to escape the recognition of this feeling of inferiority, and, therefore, now and again they appear in a social form. In other cases it is a constitutional factor (the strength

21 With striking frequency, we find youthful suicide as the culmination of a vain struggle against obsessive masturbation, which, in apparently convincing fashion, impresses the victim with the feeling of his own helplessness. In a similar fashion, the difficulties of menstruation reinforce "the debased feeling of femininity" in women. As is generally known, during this period nervous difficulties are intensified and the number of suicides increases, which provides a clear confirmation of the above observations.

of the aggressive drive), or the force of example, that points the way. The results of "heredity" can be prevented in the same way as the manifestations themselves—through psychoanalysis. It lays bare the childish feeling of inferiority, reduces it from its exaggerated state to its proper dimensions by correcting false estimates, and subordinates the revolt of masculine protest to the guidance of the expanded consciousness. *Suicide and neurosis are both childish forms of reaction to a childish overestimation of motives, humiliations, and disappointments. And so suicide represents—like neurosis and psychosis—an escape by antisocial means from the injustices of life.*

DR. MOLITOR

The question of student suicide is of great importance for teachers, not merely because of the shattering impression made by the individual cases in which children or adolescents put an end to their lives, but also in a much wider sense. It has already been pointed out in this discussion that for each successful case of suicide there is an incomparably greater number of cases in which similar circumstances have led to nervous illnesses or psychological depression of longer or shorter duration. If, therefore, the study of suicide yields practical pedagogical advice, this would benefit not only a few particularly vulnerable cases, but a great many persons, and our educational system as a whole.

The relations between the educational system and suicide have already been discussed here in a thorough and interesting fashion. As was to be expected, the discussion has pointed up the superficiality and stupidity of the judgments of dilettante pedagogues who find a ready audience in some newspapers. They assume that the teacher is at fault in every case of schoolboy suicide, and charge him with murder, or at least manslaughter. The question of individual responsibility must be carefully examined in every case, and this is, in fact, always done; but on the face of it, individual responsibility is unlikely. What the statistics refer to as "the motive" of a suicide is usually no more than the triggering factor. Such factors, as revealed by examination of individual cases, may well be poor grades or failure to graduate, which are so inevitable in our educational system, and probably in any other, that they can be predicted statistically.

But this assertion does not settle the matter

for the educator; it only states the problem. If the relationship between student suicide and the educational system were really as simple as is sometimes suggested, we could solve the problem by disciplinary reform and the attentions of the public prosecutor. In actuality, the situation is far more involved.

In dealing with the problem we can distinguish between two questions. We have already seen that school experiences will lead to suicide only in the case of individuals who are already under severe psychological stress before the concrete event. This raises the question: does our educational system intensify this psychological stress? Dr. Sadger has already pointed out that the school can be supportive, and that the relationship to the school and to the teacher can sometimes help a boy. This raises the second question: does our present educational system utilize this supportive potential to its fullest extent?

Beyond all doubt, the first question must be answered in the affirmative. Professor Freud has urged that the school treat the boy better than life will treat the man, and that the same demands not be made on boys as on adults. The existing situation is very different: the school often makes greater demands on the student

[123]

than an adult could ever bear, except in extreme circumstances. Our present system of classification, with its trilogy of individual marks, examination results, and end-of-term reports, represents formal documentation and official confirmation of failure, which can become psychological torture for the less talented boy. (This is, of course, not the normal case.) This state of affairs does not leave even the adults untouched; there are whole families who suffer from a positive school neurosis, in which the results of a Latin examination can elicit floods of joy or despair.

These are the conditions which produce the violent attacks on our educational system. And yet they are really unjust. It is not the educational system as such which creates these conditions, but the role society calls upon the school to play. Our educational system is only secondarily educational; *it is primarily an institution for the attainment of privileges.* There is a growing tendency to make the matriculation results the condition *sine qua non* for every higher career, even for quite subordinate employment in the civil service, and in large firms and commercial undertakings (the railways, etc.). The basic rationale is quite clear: the middle and upper strata of our society thereby want to secure their sons the greatest possible number of places at the feeding trough. In fact, many a young man has the greater part of his life's work behind him once he has successfully passed his matriculation. The rest is left in the hands of an uncle or godfather. But this thoughtful arrangement contains a terrible revenge: the natural significance of childhood and adolescence is replaced by an artificial and unhealthy one. The important thing is not how the individual develops in this period, but what he achieves—and often in areas that are remote from the tasks he will subsequently have to perform.

Here lie the roots of the trouble. This system of privilege imposes an unhealthy character on our educational system. It turns the teacher into an instrument for social selection and compels him to be strict, even harsh. If he is not, it means that only the social position of the parents counts and not the talent and capacities of the boy. This puts the teacher in an ambiguous position toward his pupils and burdens him with a dual role: on the one hand, he is expected to be a friend and teacher, and on the other, he has to be a judge and representative of the authorities. It poisons his relationship to the parents of his pupils, who are rarely completely frank in their dealings with the man who is in a unique position to help or harm their child. It often makes the teacher into a "trainer" who urges on the less talented pupils to ever greater efforts in order to spare them the disaster of failure. The untalented pupil is pushed through his examinations at all cost.

Let me mention in passing that the situation is worsened by the fact that the school has become a mass institution, and that in certain areas—Vienna for one—our schools are usually greatly overcrowded. This makes it difficult for the teachers to manage the curriculum, it increases unhealthy competition for places, and often demands the imposition of a discipline which even the teachers themselves find unnaturally rigid. At the same time, it makes any individual treatment of the pupils practically impossible; and as regards individual treatment of a slow pupil, the class is likely to perceive it as unjust favoritism.

How much nervous children can suffer under such school conditions—even if the teacher is well-meaning and just—and how dangerous the whole situation can become, is made particularly clear to us when we remember what Dr. Adler has to say about the role played by the feeling of inferiority in psychological crises. It cannot be denied that our present educational system quite automatically tends to reinforce this feeling of inferiority, and that instead of encouraging self-confidence, it tends to undermine it. This is due to the existing situation and certainly not to the teachers who, no matter how capable and understanding, can do no more than ameliorate the situation. Governmental school-reform measures cannot help. However well-meaning, their proposals are frequently superficial and illogical, and they are primarily intended to divert the attention of the general public from the fact that our educational system is being starved for funds—e.g., the overcrowding in our schools has been a scandal for years. The abolition of the privilege system is wholly out of the question. When the subject is touched upon at all, it is only in order to make minor alterations in the distribution of benefits, and not to abolish a situation in which the competence of a grown man will be judged by his school performance, often many decades earlier.

The deplorable effect of these abuses inherent in our educational system is intensified by psychological attitudes of both parents and teachers. Far too much importance is attached to the report card, and this importance is still

[127]

further exaggerated by many parents. It is deplorable and quite grotesque that so many parents should regard an examination failure as a disaster—which they are inclined to do even when the failure means only that they must keep their son at school for another year and does not represent a great economic burden. Nothing is more typical of the civil-service mentality that dominates our lives than the common complaint that "the boy will lose a year." This may be true for the future length-of-service bonus, but it certainly is not true in terms of the boy's physical and intellectual development. On the contrary, a year or more is added to his youth, and he has that much more time in which to develop, instead of being rushed from class to class, only to suffer failure in the end. Then the long-feared catastrophe comes about at a time when the boy is already used to lagging behind and when, for technical reasons, the advantages of repeating a class are greatly outweighed by its disadvantages. A little enlightenment of the parents in this matter would spare their children a good deal of anxiety and do away with much of the foreboding attached to the "bad report." The situation is even worse, more dangerous, when parents force their children to carry on in a course of study despite the child's repeated and clearly expressed repugnance. Failure in the upper classes of our secondary schools is, of course, a different matter; then the boy longs with all his might to be done with school, and the idea of staying on another year in conditions which have become psychologically repugnant to him is so distasteful that, in certain circumstances, it can develop into a crisis.

The teacher who regards the failure of a certain proportion of his class as something normal and statistically predictable, may fail to realize how very differently his pupils will perceive and explain the same phenomenon. Sometimes teachers tend to underline and even exaggerate the seriousness of failure—this in the interest of their pedagogic objective. Generally speaking, we can say that, from the standpoint of discipline and teaching, those pupils who are most capable of resistance and calm in face of disciplinary measures will cause their teachers most trouble. They are the ones who give the teacher his image of the class as a whole, and this image will determine the tone he adopts toward his pupils; in consequence, he will treat sensitive boys rather more roughly than is good for them, merely because he is not conscious of the effect his words will have on them.

We must also not overlook the fact that, only too often, a feeling of inferiority is deliberately and systematically induced on the basis of "ethical principles." All those who would like to turn the school into an instrument of political and religious reaction insist that its main objective should be to educate its pupils "to obedience," and the extreme representatives of this tendency deliberately set out to break the individual will. As an example of this, allow me to mention the rules and regulations in force at some schools in the provinces; they deliberately encroach on the private lives of their pupils, and one can see no other purpose than the intention of making the boys feel their lack of freedom all the more keenly. "Boys must learn to obey." The treatment of students is only a repetition of what the teachers themselves had to endure in their schooldays. For this reason, the growing attempts at professional organization among our teachers can only be regarded as a real blessing for the school, since it provides the teacher with a backbone, so that, being free and independent himself, he will want to educate others in the same way. In every sadist there is something of a masochist.

The subject of our discussion has made me dwell at length on the less pleasing aspects of our educational system. But I do not want to create the impression that these aspects are predominant. On the contrary, I am firmly convinced that school life is essentially supportive, and that the positive effects are increasing even if they are not always allowed free play. I agree with Dr. Sadger and Professor Freud that the school offers a boy important personal contacts, that it nourishes his active and passive need for love, and that it allows his emotional life to expand beyond the limits of the home. During periods of temporary or permanent estrangement between him and his family, he will find substitutes at school, in a form that is particularly favorable because a superficial relationship is established among a large number of individuals, while it remains open to each to establish intimate relationships with particular individuals. In other words, "the compulsion to love" which prevails in the family is absent in the school. The operation of this substitute function of the school can be seen from the fact that the boy's love for his family and his attachment to the school are usually in inverse ratio— "mother's boys" are usually poor school friends, and whoever still sees an ideal in his father will not look for one in his teacher.

From what I have said, you will see that I regard a boy's relationship to his fellow pupils to be as important as his relationship to his teachers. The former leadership relationship of the father can be transferred, at least to some extent, to the older and more precocious schoolmates.

Now what effect do our educational institutions have on the relationship of the pupils to each other? In some respects, their influence is positively deleterious. The approval of tale-bearing can be regarded as a thing of the past; but the examination system with its competitive atmosphere still exists, encouraging envy and jealousy on the one hand, and arrogance and self-righteousness on the other. But I consider it most important that today the relationship among the pupils develops spontaneously, without positive influence from the teacher, since it develops largely in leisure hours outside the school, or in the recreational breaks, when the teacher is present only as a passive supervisor. The fact that, in consequence, individuals of doubtful quality can often play at least a temporary leading role is a lesser evil. The crucial factor, for us, is that the types described by Dr. Adler, who have the greatest need of comradeship, are unable to make the necessary contact; in fact, their inadequacy and shyness often make them a target for mockery. In this way a new and fateful factor can enter into their development. Nowadays, a teacher can intervene only occasionally and not very effectively. We shall see real progress only when the school becomes a recreational community as well as a working community.

In this respect, the modern encouragement of organized games—even if it looks more impressive on paper than it is in reality—is a very hopeful beginning. Unfortunately, however, the personal relationship between those who take part recedes almost completely into the background; and since the matter is left in the hands of the gymnastics teacher or another teacher who hardly knows the boys, the purely technical aspect of the game will be given greatest emphasis. The only games and sports that are likely to serve our purpose are those that promote real social contacts, such as hikes and rowing parties, in which the teachers who usually work with the boys take a positive and not merely a passive role. School outings, which are, unfortunately, few and far between, have a most favorable influence on both students and teachers.

I hardly need stress that this extension of the school into a recreational community would fundamentally change the relationship between pupil and teacher and considerably reduce the emotional distance between them. Although promising beginnings have been made, I have little hope that a great deal will be done in this direction, since any kind of educational reform costs money. As long as our educational authorities rely on the "idealism" of our teachers for these noncurricular activities instead of incorporating them into the curriculum and paying for them, this part of the educational activity will not generally be carried out with the necessary enthusiasm and energy. For one thing, most teachers in our big towns are compelled to take on extra, time-consuming work in order to supplement their meager incomes.

With this we have arrived at one of the weakest points of our educational system. To take a real interest in a hundred or more youngsters, if only briefly, takes time; and our teachers never have time. They do not have time outside the classroom because they are victims of the wholesale paper-grading lunacy, and any spare time is taken up to the point of exhaustion by other work. They have no time during school hours because a constantly expanding curriculum has to be mastered in shortened lesson and homework hours. Apart from intensified tension in school life, the result of all this is that the teaching of many subjects is becoming a chase, and the teacher is never free of anxiety that there will not be enough time to cover the material. On the one hand, this does lead to a more effective use of the time available, and encourages the development of didactic ability; but on the other hand, the teacher, who should direct himself to the student as a whole, tends to disappear behind the mere educational technician. Since he has no time for the individual, he begins to work more and more with that abstraction, "the class." His natural ambition is to achieve a high standard with "his class." When he finds that a slow pupil resists his attempts to carry him along, he soon begins to feel an understandable desire to get rid of the boy before he "lowers the general level." Unfortunately, this can make even a dedicated teacher, who is kind to his pupils on the whole, very harsh toward the unfortunate individual.

This seems to me to be the reason why teachers of the quality desired by Professor Freud are very rare today. Their whole situation and the nature of the educational system pushes our teachers in the opposite direction. The often-heard opinion that all the troubles of our schools really arise from the incompetence of the teachers reflects a correct observation based

[135]

on a false explanation. Of course, even today a first-class teaching talent can find a fruitful field of activity, but the point is that a mass institution like the modern school cannot demand exceptional talents from the teaching staff. Its atmosphere and organization must be such that the teacher of average talent can carry out his work competently.

Although my observations have, of necessity, touched on many aspects of school life, I do not think that I have been guilty of any real deviation from our point. Whether the school encourages or hampers its pupils psychologically depends on a variety of factors. At this point, we must ask ourselves whether suicide prophylaxis in the more restricted sense of the term is at all possible through the school. In this connection I wish to make it very clear that I am opposed to the mechanical prophylaxis that has been tried in Vienna, in which "bad reports" are no longer given to pupils regarded as "suicide subjects," and their parents are asked to come and collect them instead. First of all, such a system involves a very real danger that those responsible will fail to recognize precisely those pupils who are most prone to suicide. Second, this positively fosters the idea that suicide is, so to speak, a normal reaction, to be expected at any time as a consequence of bad report cards. This can only give the idea of suicide a renewed suggestive force and, in some boys, even arouse an idea that was previously dormant. It is precisely the suggestive effect that makes every successful suicide such a great danger. We often find that someone who has long nourished the idea of suicide finally carries it out only when he has found someone to imitate. This warns us that the investigation of a suicide by the school authorities must be carried out with the utmost tact and circumspection, especially its discussion in the press. The sensational fashion in which so many newspapers present such news, and the aura of martyrdom they delight in placing around these unfortunates, can all too easily induce another victim to follow the fatal example. This does not mean that there should not be the freest possible public discussion, or that school conditions should not be subjected to stern criticism where such criticism seems called for; but it does mean that anyone conscious of his responsibility should say what he feels he must say without focusing the spotlight of scandal on the unfortunate affair. If we do not place confidence in mechanical prophylaxis, a wise teacher may well be able to take effective precautionary measures in good time.

Very often defiance and a desire to take revenge (on parents or teachers) are the real motives for suicide. But it cannot be assumed that there is any objective justification for these feelings. Rather, such motivation suggests that the person concerned stood very close to the suicide's heart. This should not make us overlook the fact that "the defiant ones" are probably just those who are least suitably treated in our schools today. Where obedience is set up as the pedagogic ideal *par excellence,* defiance is naturally regarded as the crime which puts the perpetrator outside the community. Generally, such reactions are often ignored as being irrelevant. Yet, in such cases, the teacher could often intervene helpfully, if he would not wait passively until the cause for defiance has passed and the reaction has died down, but work actively to re-establish the friendly contact. Naturally, the healing balm must not take the form of abandoning any part of the teacher's authority, or toning down a well-merited rebuke. It must consist in letting the boy see that his teacher feels a personal interest in him.

A teacher who makes a habit of observing his pupils closely will soon recognize the type Dr. Adler has described to us as being particularly endangered. The first indications he will notice will be awkwardness, embarrassment, shyness, and unmotivated blushing. A particularly characteristic sign is the apparently contradictory combination of stressed laziness and indifference with excessive sensitiveness. In such cases a thorough discussion with the boy's parents, not confined to his educational activities but taking in his personal character, can frequently do a great deal of good. It is very often particularly necessary because such a pupil will tend to present a very different picture of himself at home than he does at school. Thus the psychologically trained eye of the professional teacher could favorably influence the boy's treatment at home.

I am very well aware that this modest attempt to adapt knowledge obtained by the psychoanalytic method to the purposes of education will not satisfy those who like their scientific conclusions clear-cut. There can be no universally applicable prophylaxis against student suicide. But whoever realizes that our knowledge must become deeper before it can become simpler will be persuaded, I am sure—not by what I have said, but by the general conclusions of the discussion—that psychoanalysis can enliven the often stagnant stream of our educational system. We have here an antidote to the super-

SIGMUND FREUD

ficiality and mechanization of the experimental method, unquestioned as is its value in the right place. We have an opportunity, indeed, the obligation, of constantly deepening our knowledge.

PROFESSOR FREUD

Gentlemen,—I have an impression that, in spite of all the valuable material that has been brought before us in this discussion, we have not reached a decision on the problem that interests us. We were anxious above all to know how it becomes possible for the extraordinarily powerful life instinct to be overcome: whether this can only come about with the help of a disappointed libido or whether the ego can renounce its self-preservation for its own egoistic motives. It may be that we have failed to answer this psychological question because we have no adequate means of approaching it. We can, I think, only take as our starting-point the condition of melancholia, which is so familiar to us clinically, and a comparison between it and the affect of mourning. The affective processes in melancholia, however, and the vicissitudes undergone by the libido in that condition, are

[140]

totally unknown to us. Nor have we arrived at a psycho-analytic understanding of the chronic affect of mourning. Let us suspend our judgment till experience has solved this problem.